More North Devon History
series two

Peter Christie

Edward Gaskell
DEVON

First published 2009
Edward Gaskell *publishers*
The Old *Gazette* Building
6 Grenville Street
Bideford
Devon
EX39 2EA

isbn   (10) 1-906769-07-9
isbn   (13) 978-1-906769-07-9

More North Devon History
series two

Typeset, printed and bound by
Lazarus Press
Caddsdown Business Park
Bideford
Devon
EX39 3DX
www. lazaruspress. com

Foreword

Last year I published a fourth volume of my historical essays entitling it *North Devon History - Series Two* (there had been three volumes in the first series). I have continued to write articles and, using these, plus collecting together more of those published in the *North Devon Journal* and the sadly defunct *Bideford Gazette*, has enabled me to put together this new book. As before there is a full index to people and places and a note as to if and where they have previously appeared. A complete list of the titles to the 879 articles published in the two local newspapers is available on the Devon section of the Genuki website for those interested.

Peter Christie

Bideford 1 May 2009

Contents

Religion

Law and Order

Odds and Ends

Dedicated to my father
Roy Christie

PEOPLE

1. Fifteenth-century North Devonians

It is a truism in history that the further back one goes the fewer records exist. Time and spring-cleaning urges have taken their toll. Luckily as a nation we haven't been invaded for over 900 years and our governments have accumulated huge collections of official records a large number of which date back many centuries.

Amongst them are the Close Rolls. Written on long rolls of parchment they record the orders sent from the monarch and his or her ministers to the various officers of state. Some 21,000 of these lists or orders survive from the years 1204 to 1903 and they contain a real hotch-potch of material including occasional references to North Devon.

Thus in 1413 John Butte was appointed as the Deputy Butler (or customs officer) for the ports of 'Tawmouth' and 'Barstable'. Such appointments are common although often they came with many other duties attached. In 1440, for example, an order was sent out to the customs official at Barnstaple that they had 'in consideration of the damage done to the king's subjects by pirates. . . to arrest [i.e. commandeer] twenty ships and ten other vessels as well as barges. . . with sufficient masters and mariners to serve the king on the sea.' This is, of course, an early example of the press gang though at this date, before there was a Royal Navy, ships had to be 'pressed' as well as men.

A similar order was recorded in 1461 when various gentlemen including Richard Chichestre, John Gyffard and the Mayor of Barnstaple were ordered 'to urge the king's subjects of the north parts of the county of Devon to supply ships well equipped with men, victuals and habiliments of war for half a year at their own expense for defence against the king's enemies.' You will notice that they were expected to pay for this loyal gesture themselves!

There were, however, rewards for successful commanders. Thus in 1462 John Fortescu and William Chicheley of Parkham were given land valued at £46 per year 'in consideration of their charges and perils incurred in the king's conflicts and battles.'

The land incidentally had come from a traitor to the king - so he wasn't being that generous.

The king kept an eye on foreigners living in the area presumably seeing them as potential spies or fifth columnists. Thus in 1436 county officers had to draw up lists of 'aliens' living in their areas and we find Henry Beremaker alias Perwarden who was born in 'Makelburgh' (possibly Germany) living in Barnstaple along with John de Bee of Brabant (Holland).

Much detail is given in the rolls on wrongdoers both civil and criminal. The civil offenders included John atte Wylle of Northam a baker who was arrested in 1434 for not appearing at court to answer a charge of owing £2 to William Saundyr. On the same list is William Podyner of Bideford a dyer who owed money to the same William, and Alexander Canderton a merchant of Pilton. Similarly in 1441 John Flogan of 'Toryton' should have appeared to answer a charge of trespassing on the property of Clarice daughter of Robert Noreys.

One criminal was William Gille of Bideford a 'shipman' who one night 'burned the house of John Smyth' along with goods valued at £5. He was arrested and taken to Exeter prison. When brought to trial he claimed to be 'guiltless'. The jury reckoned he was 'beside himself' i.e. insane and that 'the felony was not done of malice' and so sent him back to prison to await the king's decision over what should happen to him. King Henry VI decided to leave him there.

These few scattered glimpses of our ancestors from some 550 years ago are fascinating and we should regard ourselves as lucky to have them - if only to bring home to us just how lucky we are to live in today's world.
North Devon Journal 25.5.1999

2. Hatherleigh's handy man
To paraphrase Wilde 'to lose one hand is unfortunate, to lose both is carelessness' - yet this is exactly what happened to one Thomas Roberts who, though handless, lead a full active life as schoolmaster of Hatherleigh for nearly 50 years.

Born at Tor Point, Cornwall in 1771 he had for his godfather Lord Graves then in charge of Plymouth Dock who, when Thomas was only 4 days old entered him in the Royal Navy as a midshipman! This wasn't as bizarre as it seems as promotion then depended on length of service and clearly if one's 'service' began as a baby you had a great advantage over later entrants.

Thomas joined Graves on his ship the 98 gun *London* in 1780 and was soon in action during the War of American Independence. During one engagement young Thomas was about to throw a grenade when it exploded destroying both of his hands and wounding him in 17 places. Treatment at that date consisted of cauterizing stumps of limbs in boiling tar - an experience Thomas survived. The ship's carpenter rigged up a wooden hand which held a pen and Thomas learnt to write again becoming the Captain's clerk.

In 1788 Thomas left the Navy and spent some time carving himself an improved set of 'hands' as well as broadening his reading. This stood him in good stead when, aged 21, Sir James Hamlyn of Clovelly hired him as tutor to his children. Whilst there Thomas both surveyed and laid out what we know today as Hobby Drive using skills picked up at sea.

Thomas stayed in Clovelly for about 8 years becoming locally famous as the 'handless teacher'. His fame spread to Hatherleigh where there was then no school. John Pearse, a prominent wool merchant, decided to remedy this and rode over to Clovelly to invite Thomas to become master at his new school. Thomas agreed and in 1797 came to Hatherleigh where the old vestry room over the gateway leading into the churchyard had been set up as a schoolroom. He didn't come alone as on the 24th of August 1797 he married Mary Ann Brent at Clovelly. The couple went on to produce ten children of whom seven reached maturity.

Thomas realised very quickly that he and his wife couldn't live on his teacher's wages and he began advertising for boarders. His fame must have been fairly great as within a few years there was 'generally an average of eighty boarders beside day scholars.' They were taught 'Mathematics, Latin, Writing, Arithmetic, Drawing etc.' The old vestry room soon proved insufficient and

Thomas purchased an old building in the centre of Hatherleigh at the junction of South, High and Higher Streets, razed it and built a new school on the site. As something of a novelty playing fields were provided whilst swimming was available in two pools in the River Lew not too far away.

Where Thomas got the money from to do this is a mystery although Lord Graves might have advanced it to him. Wherever it came from the investment was well-made and Thomas ran the school until 1845 - nearly 50 years of service. It is recorded that 'During this period he educated upwards of eighteen hundred youths, boarders in his house.' It was also noted that 'amongst this large number of boys and during this extended period of time, not a boy died at the school' which reads rather oddly today.

In intervals between teaching Thomas continued an active life turning out many ship models, produced chess sets on a lathe and even carved himself a whole series of different 'hands' suitable for different jobs. He was an 'enthusiastic sportsman' shooting over Hatherleigh Moor and a keen fisherman who somehow tied his own flies. He also, at various times filled the office of Overseer of the Poor, Church-warden, Surveyor of the Highways and Portreeve (equivalent of a Mayor) of the town.

His wife died in December 1845 aged 72 and Thomas decided to retire. He lived another three years dying in December 1848 and was buried next to his wife in Hatherleigh churchyard. His memory was kept alive by three things; a local pond he built to sail his model boats on and teach his pupils navigation known as 'Roberts' Pond', a gallery in the North aisle of Hatherleigh church which he erected at his own expense in 1814 and the 1800 or so pupils he had taught. Perhaps the best lesson he ever gave, however, was the one he gave to everyone - that a seemingly crippling disability could be overcome if one tried hard enough. *North Devon Journal* 5.11.1998

3. The Matron

A little while ago I recounted the sad story of the Secretary and Chief Surgeon of the North Devon Infirmary in Barnstaple who committed suicide in 1838 when his thieving from the hospital coffers was on the point of exposure. The management committee decided from thenceforward to separate the two posts. This they thought would make future fraud impossible, restore the public's trust in the organisation and thus maintain the flow of charitable donations. Sadly another scandal soon burst upon them.

The story begins in November 1846 when the then Matron resigned. A special meeting 'of the Benefactors and Subscribers' was called to elect a new woman to the job. It was specified that candidates had to be aged between 30 and 50, have 'a competent knowledge of housekeeping', be 'of unexceptionable moral character' and have no 'encumbrance' i.e. family. This paragon was to be paid £20 a year plus board and lodging.

As was common at that date hopefuls took out advertisements in the *Journal* seeking the votes of the committee members - and amongst these was Sarah Miller of Barnstaple who, in due course, was appointed to the post. She was the daughter of 'a former hostess of the Britannia at Ilfracombe' who for many years had nursed her sick mother. On a ballot being taken she received 231 votes against 93 for the only other candidate.

After her appointment she again used an advertisement to thank the Committee saying, 'It will be my constant and most assiduous exertion to fulfil the duties of my office and the satisfaction of the managers of the institution, and the comfort of the patients.' Employees knew their place in those days.

All went well for the first few months but in February 1847 Sarah abruptly resigned. This followed the discovery that 'she had induced the butchers, who supplied the institution, to send in false bills' and had been quietly pocketing the difference between these and the real bills.

The embarrassed committee members who had supported her nomination expressed their 'extreme disappointment' at the way she had behaved and then proposed to elect a new Matron 'from the better walks of life.' Indeed one member requested that the job description specified that the applicants had to be a 'gentlewoman' but the Chairman 'did not think it expedient to put forward in the advertisement any such restrictions as to class, the precise meaning of which it might afterwards be a little difficult to define.'

In fact four women applied but one was excluded on the basis of 'having been lately left a widow with one child.' The successful candidate this time was a Mrs.Hawkins from Torrington whose nursing experience came from looking after her sick husband. More importantly the ladies on the hospital committee 'would be happy in having as the matron a person with whom they could freely communicate' - i.e. one of the same social class as themselves.

On this basis she was appointed and so the troubled Infirmary settled back into normalcy going about its job of looking after the sick and ill of North Devon. Looking back we can only consider what a wonderful cameo of human frailty and snobbery the case displays.

North Devon Journal 25.3.1999

4. Conjugal celebrations at Clovelly

To most of us our wedding day is one of the most important and nerve wracking events of our life. Imagine, however, if an entire village turned out to help you celebrate it! In April 1850 Major Henry Fane of the 4th Dragoon Guards married the eldest daughter of Sir James and Lady Mary Hamlyn Williams the owners of Clovelly - and the associated celebrations ran over two days.

On the day of the marriage, which was held in London, the morning began in Clovelly with the firing of cannons and the ringing of church bells. Every cottage was festooned with flags 'bearing appropriate mottoes' whilst arches of evergreen branches were erected across the narrow streets. Sir James laid on a meal at the New Inn for all the tradesmen and labourers employed on his estate which consisted of 'prime pieces of beef, mutton, hams, and plum pudding, with plenty of good old ale.' Here numerous toasts were drunk and 'much hilarity' was seen.

The really big celebration, however, occurred the following day when the two newly-weds arrived to spend their honeymoon in Clovelly. The morning again began with the firing of cannon and pealing of church bells - which continued all day. All the boats in the harbour were 'gaily decorated with various flags and bunting.' All during the day the local people streamed into the village so that by 4 p.m. there were upwards of 2000 collected at the end of Hobby Drive. At 4.45 the carriage carrying the honeymooners came down the road to be met by Mr.Dannell the village schoolmaster who read out an 'address' on behalf of the community.

After a flowery opening the speech got even more sugary, 'Honoured Madam, and you honourable Sir! We heartily and gladly welcome you. We beg to assure you that it is our earnest desire that your married life, commenced under such happy auspices, may be abundantly blessed.' He continued in this vein for some time and when he finished the couple 'bowed respectfully to the assembly, and returned thanks.' This was greeted with 'tremendous cheering which was distinctly heard for many miles.' The local band then struck up 'Haste to the Wedding' and the huge crowd proceeded to Clovelly Court where 'the large gothic arch' at the entrance had been covered in evergreen boughs and flowers.

The procession was led by the carriage which was being pulled by young men, the horses having been taken out. This was followed by 'four young Nymphs' dressed in white with their hair garlanded with flowers who were carrying a 'snow-white banner' bearing the embroidered words 'Long may you live and happy may you be.' They arrived at the Court 'amidst the firing of mortars and cannon' set out on the lawn whilst the band now played 'Home, Sweet Home'. As the couple got down from their carriage the local uniformed coastguards 'presented arms' and fired several salvoes in their honour.

In the evening many hundreds of guests assembled on the lawn to watch fireworks and be serenaded by the band. From 8 pm until midnight every cottage in the village 'was brilliantly illuminated' which 'from its romantic situation must have been seen to great advantage from vessels passing up and down the bay.'

This being Victorian Britain a strong moral message was drawn from the proceedings. The *Journal's* correspondent point-

ed out that the celebrations were so successful due to the village's owner having constantly practiced 'good, noble and kind actions' for his tenants. Apparently the poor and those in ill-health could always count on his support and the 'genuine kindness of this truly excellent family.' Indeed the whole event with its 'spontaneous exhibition of genuine affection' proved the old adage 'As ye sow, so shall ye reap.'
North Devon Journal 11.11.1999

5. Weare Giffard goldseekers

Emigration from Britain was extremely widespread in the nineteenth century and North Devon sent its fair share of people abroad. Most went in search of a better life with high hopes of making their fortune. Many made a success of their new life but few made fortunes. In the 1850s, however, gold was discovered in Australia and the promise of a quick killing lured many.

In 1854 two young men, John Davy and Thomas Harris, were living in Weare Giffard when they 'took it into their heads to set off on a sixteen thousand mile trip to the gold diggings of South Australia.' Most such hopefuls were soon disillusioned by the backbreaking work and poor returns. John and Thomas, however, were among those select few who literally struck gold.

Just nine months after they arrived in Australia, they were excavating a trial hole when their picks hit a large nugget of gold. On cleaning and weighing it they were astonished to find that it weighed 84lbs. The discovery drew hundreds of other miners who marvelled at the size and purity of the find.

The two young men lost no time in moving their find to Melbourne and from there to Hobart where they went with it on a ship bound for Liverpool. Arriving home in Britain they were quickly offered huge sums of money for the nugget eventually accepting one of £4,085 - and this at a time when the average North Devon labourer was earning just 10/- (50p) a week.

The *Journal* reported all this in some detail adding that John and Thomas came back to Weare Giffard in July 1855 to be met by a large crowd of well-wishers and the curious. The church bells rang out for the first time since the two had left for

Australia - as they, along with a brother of one of them who had also gone gold-hunting, were the village bell-ringers!

John and Thomas may have returned home in triumph but only a few weeks later the *Journal* was reporting a rather different story about John. He was up before the magistrates at Torrington Petty Sessions court to answer a charge of fathering an illegitimate child on Mary Ann Fry of Weare Giffard. At this date a woman who found herself pregnant and unmarried had to appear in court to swear who the father was - and he would be ordered to pay a weekly sum for upkeep of the child.

The reporter covering the trial clearly enjoyed wordplay as his story refers to the finding of the gold and then says that 'when he (John) returned to his own native home he discovered another 'nugget' far more precious than the one he found in Australia.'

John denied paternity and produced nine witnesses to say he wasn't the father but Mary Ann 'passed through the ordeal of the law and the lawyers without any stain being proved on her character, except that which the defendant himself had stamped there.'

The local fame of the defendant had attracted a vast crowd of some 300 people who squashed into the small court room to hear the proceedings. In cases like this when the magistrates accepted the woman's evidence (this was of course before DNA testing) they would order the father to pay 1/6 (7.5p) a week to the mother for the upkeep of the child until the age of 14 or 16. In this case they accepted Mary Ann's version of events and imposed an order of 2/- (10p) per week on her lover - which seems remarkably low given his new-found wealth. Such is life!
North Devon Journal 26.4.2001

6. Become Barnstaple's MP for £75,000

The secrecy of the polling booth is something we take for granted today - indeed it is one of the greatest freedoms we possess. In the past, however, public voting was the rule and as a consequence corruption was rife as would-be vote buyers could see which way you voted and then pay you a cash sum agreed before-hand.

Nowhere was this more true than in Barnstaple where things got so bad that in 1854, following a particularly 'dirty' election two years before, a Parliamentary Commission was sent to the town to carry out a searching inquiry. The evidence they collected filled 516 foolscap pages and makes incredible reading today.

Baldly stated, of the 696 men who cast their votes some 256 had been bribed - some 251 of whom voted for the Conservatives Sir William Fraser and Richard Bremridge and 5 who voted for the Liberal Lord Ebrington. The estimated cost of the bribes came to £1830 (worth some £75,000 at modern prices) being in the form of cash payments plus beer in local pubs.

The system was simplicity itself. Conservative agents would approach electors and extract a promise of their vote. Afterwards 'the wife of the voter. . . would find £6 in a very mysterious manner upon her table; about it as little as possible was said by her to her husband.'

The Commission Report is full of the fascinating evidence from numerous voters and election officials. Thus the Mayor and editor of the *Journal* William Avery admitted that when the Liberal candidate first approached him about standing in Barnstaple he 'had no hesitation in at once advising his Lordship not to come to Barnstaple as he knew how corrupt the town was.'

The Town Clerk Lionel Bencraft recounted how he had seen drunken electors, accompanied by Conservative canvassers, taken to the polling room and cast their votes publicly for the Conservative candidates. Unfortunately he also had to admit that he himself served on the Liberal election committee - an admission he followed with a lot of shifty answers about the free availability of wine at his party's committee rooms.

Some of the witnesses were more open. George Gaydon, a grocer, was positively proud of his corruption and even produced a list of those to whom he had given £6 each as a 'gift' from the Conservatives. Of the 15 recipients 12 were called Gaydon! The £90 he had paid out came from a John Petter a local ironmonger and the apparent 'paymaster' for his party.

When this Petter was questioned he was asked 'Your name is rather celebrated in the electioneering annals of the town'? to which he replied 'It is'. When pressed for details about his bribing activities he could only say, 'I must tell you, that from the great interest I felt in the election I was extremely excited. I had not slept for many nights, feeling such an interest in the matter, and I was quite worn out with fatigue, and only kept up by excitement, so that I cannot fix my memory with everything which occurred.' Remarkably he had forgotten ever bribing anyone! Luckily lots of the bribed electors clearly recalled receiving money from him.

It was these sorts of lies and obfuscations that caused the Commissioners to write in their Report that 'in some instances our efforts to elicit the truth were met with gross evasion, prevarication, and even perjury, rendered still more deplorable by the shameless bearing of those who had recourse to them.'

The outcome of all this inquiry was that Bremridge and Fraser were unseated and a Barnstaple Bribery Prevention Bill was introduced into Parliament to prevent further abuses.

This was never passed, however, and in August 1854 a new election was held when two new Conservatives were elected - though on a reduced majority. One of these, however, was unseated the next year for corruption. Indeed over the next 20 years until the first election by secret ballot in 1874 bribery continued to be rife in the town. It was only these secret ballots that effectively stopped bribery in Barnstaple - after all why bribe someone when you couldn't be certain they had voted for you? *North Devon Journal* 26.8.1999

7. Witchery in Barnstaple

One of the things I have often written about are the folklore beliefs of North Devonians in the past. We still have many of these beliefs today, for example, lucky horseshoes and astrology to name but two but I suspect few people still believe in the reality of witchcraft. Actually claiming to be a witch hasn't been a crime for nearly 80 years of course but in the nineteenth century locals could still be found who firmly believed in the objective power of witches - as is shown by a report in the *Journal* from May 1870.

The Barnstaple magistrates must have been surprised when

Philip Burch of Trinity Street appeared before them on a charge of assaulting Mary Ann Sampson for having tormented him with witchcraft. Philip was fairly well-known in the town as he had been one of those implicated in the infamous bribery cases that were a hallmark of Barnstaple parliamentary elections for so many years. Indeed the *Journal* report refers to him under his nickname 'Manager Burch' which alludes to his part in the buying of votes.

As to the assault charge Mary had been in the Pannier Market one Thursday (the next day was Good Friday and the market had been brought forward a day) when Burch came up to her, took a needle from his sleeve and severely scratched her arm with it. As she said 'It bled very much and the mark is still there' (this was a fortnight later). She claimed to have given him no provocation adding she had 'never spoke an angry word to the man in my lifetime.'

After the attack she had gone to the police station and seen P.c.Molland who advised her to summons Burch. The policeman seems to have gone with her to confront Burch as, in the presence of the officer, 'Burch said he would do it again' claiming 'that I had had power over him long enough, and he would stand it no longer.'

In court Burch was called on to explain his rather cryptic comment. He began by saying when he gave her the scratch she exclaimed 'You bad man, what did you do that for?' and he had answered 'You know what 'tis for, well enough.'

This obviously didn't answer the magistrates' question and Burch went on to say 'Gentlemen, I have suffered five year's affliction from her; I have been under her power, and more than a hundred people advised me to fetch the blood of that woman to destroy the spell.' Such a belief goes back a long way and, indeed, was one of the best known 'cures' for bewitchment.

With a touch of bathos, which caused laughter in court, Philip ended his defence by saying 'I have lost 14 canaries and from 40 to 50 goldfinches; as fast as I got them they died' - adding that at one time he had been the subject of five legal actions against him all of which he seemed to blame on Mary's malign powers. The Mayor, who was the chief magistrate, could only say 'it was most extraordinary that such ignorance and superstition should prevail in the present enlightened age.' Speaking for himself 'He had hoped that long ere this such absurd nonsense had been banished.'

The bench thought the assault had been clearly proved and so fined Philip 2/6 (12.5p) - and if he couldn't pay then he was to be gaoled for a week. Sadly Philip, who was receiving 'parish relief' or the dole, had no money and so was hauled off to gaol. Arriving there he remarked that he 'was quite indifferent about a week's confinement' as he had the satisfaction of knowing 'he had conquered the devil' and that his life would be much better from now on. Rather unfortunately within three weeks the *Journal* was reporting his death - so perhaps his belief in Mary Ann's powers wasn't quite so eccentric as we might think?

8. 'There's no such fool as an old fool'

In 1857 the Divorce Act was passed in England and Wales which for the first time allowed unhappy partners to both separate and remarry. Prior to this couples who split up were not legally allowed to remarry. Divorces were very rare for the first few decades after the passing of the Act but one notorious attempt to obtain one occurred in August 1870. Heard in Westminster before a judge and 'Special Jury' one Gilbert Babbage charged his wife Charlotte with committing adultery with two men.

Gilbert was a 50 year old widower with an extensive cattle and butchery business in Mariansleigh who had met and married 20 year old Charlotte White. His evidence began with the statement that the marriage hadn't worked as her behaviour was 'exceedingly violent and improper.' Indeed it was only 6 weeks after the wedding that she became 'rusty'.

In August 1869 she announced she was off to the Tiverton Races and despite his remonstrations she did go. After 4 days she returned saying 'she had met with a very good tempered gentleman' who had offered to maintain her. She then became abusive and Gilbert decided discretion was the better part of valour and kept quiet.

On another occasion he had been away on business and Henry Manning, a farmer of Chittlehampton, visited Charlotte. Gilbert later found the pair having tea together in the George Hotel in South Molton one market day. He later told her that he didn't like her talking to a married man to which she replied 'I am **** if I shall not talk to him, if I think proper; you shall never be master over me.' Naively he added that 'she has always been exceedingly anxious to go to Southmolton market on Saturdays and I could not make it out.'

Gilbert's breaking point came when he was told by some acquaintances that Charlotte had been seen kissing Manning in a secluded corner of South Molton cemetery. Attending South Molton market a few days later all his fellow farmers were openly gossiping about Charlotte having slept with Edwin Holmes - one of Gilbert's servants! This was the last straw and the cuckolded husband moved into a separate bedroom and barred his door at night as he was frightened Charlotte would attack him after he announced his intention of divorcing her.

Cross-examined he denied ever beating or insulting his wife but became rather shifty when asked if he had been unfaithful both to Charlotte and to his first wife. He said nothing at all when accused of fathering a child on a local married woman called Smith. This Mrs.Smith had been in the habit of abusing Charlotte and crowing over her intimacy with Gilbert whenever she saw her rival. When asked if Charlotte took to drink because of his treatment of her he gave the ambiguous answer 'I could not keep her from drink'.

Various witnesses were called including Caroline Milton a servant of Babbage who gave evidence that her fellow servant Holmes usually slept with Mrs.Babbage whenever her husband was attending Exeter Market. Another servant Elizabeth Harris recorded how Manning had also stayed overnight with Mrs.Babbage and how her mistress had instructed her to say nothing about it to her master. Another 5 witnesses including a local policeman gave supporting evidence.

Charlotte was then examined at length and denied all the charges, her evidence being corroborated by her mother. Manning also appeared and denied the existence of any affair between him and Charlotte although he did admit he had kissed her once in the churchyard but that 'she kicked up a fuss about it' and so he didn't try again.

The case took two days to hear and at the end the judge summed up and the jury took just 30 minutes to find Charlotte 'Not Guilty on all the issues'. Divorce may have been legalised but clearly it still wasn't easy to get one!
North Devon Journal 23.9.1999

9. Mock Mayors in South Molton

I have written before about the curious old custom of electing 'mock mayors' in North Devon. Seen as a spoof on the real thing their election was an opportunity for a drunken spree and sometimes acerbic political point scoring. I knew of such events in Bideford, Barnstaple, Torrington, Buckland Brewer, Parracombe and Appledore but can now add South Molton to that list.

In March 1912 a group of local men met at the Tiverton Inn for a 'smoking concert and social evening' at the invite of the 'Mayor and Corporation of Derby, South Molton.' The newspaper reporter who covered this meeting noted that 'This mock civil body, which is composed of representatives of the artisan class conducts its proceedings with much dignity.' The 'Mayor' was named as T.Chanter, seven 'councillors' were also listed along with J.Gregory the 'Town Clerk' and Mr.Everest the Medical Officer of Health. The 'Mayor' had a robe and chain of office and was attended by a beadle in full uniform - so clearly the event was taken seriously even if it was only for fun.

The evening opened with the 'Mayor' talking about the 'arduous duties' they were expected to perform but he promised to try his best. Another of the members, T.Willmetts, then denounced those who thought the 'primary motive' of his 'council' was 'enjoyment'. In fact they were embodied in order 'to check the action of other public bodies who might in ignorance carry out schemes which would prove detrimental to the inhabitants.' This of course was a thinly veiled comment on the real council.

He went on to point out that he and his fellow 'councillors' were 'not like the others who were the custodians of the ratepayers' purse' in that if money was needed they did not go to the ratepayers for it but rather found it from their own pockets. He reckoned this to be 'an excellent manner to prevent reckless expenditure.' How true - and one wonders what would happen if the same method of financing council operations was introduced today?

The 'Mayor' thanked Mr.Willmets, said he thought it a great privilege to be in office and ended with the slightly cryptic remark that 'he had always endeavoured to do what was right, and not to please anyone.' His last act was to begin the musical programme which consisted of songs by various 'councillors', a duet on banjo and whistle and even 'several gramophone selections.'

At the end of all this jollity the 'Ex-Mayor' proposed a vote of thanks to the new 'Mayor' and reckoned that such evenings would be 'a great inducement to the members of the Council to continue the efforts they had already put forward for the advantage of the ratepayers.' On that note and following the singing of the National Anthem this most convivial of councils broke up and went home.

The presence of an 'Ex-Mayor' suggests that the event wasn't just a one-off. Given the date I suspect the First World War probably put an end to these occasions but I would be intrigued to know if anyone remembers them or when they finished.
North Devon Journal 4.3.1999

10 The wise woman of Bideford

Most people today, if asked, would deny they believe in occult forces - yet how many read their astrological forecast in the newspapers or have some odd system for choosing their Lottery numbers? Many of us have a strange fascination for these odd beliefs - a fascination that others have used to exploit or dupe us. In April 1901 a case came up for trial at the Bideford Borough Police Court which demonstrated how this type of exploitation might occur.

William Hewitt was a labourer living at Slade, Ilfracombe whose father John had been ill for some time and showed no signs of recovering. In February 1901 he made a trip to Silver Street in Bideford to see a widow called Sarah Sayers. Her first words to him were, eerily, 'I am expecting you'. He told her about his 60 year old father whom he reckoned had been 'overlooked' (the target of black magic).

Sarah then got him to cut a pack of cards into three parts. Lifting the top card she said it showed his father had been 'overlooked' by a man whilst the second card showed a woman was also involved. She then said 'I can cure him, and it will cost £2. 2s.' William agreed to pay whereupon, and presumably realising she was dealing with a sucker, she added 'You are ill-wished too, and it will cost a guinea to cure you' - a charge William also agreed to pay.

A few days later Sarah travelled to Ilfracombe and gave the family some 'bags' to wear around their necks with the instruction 'they must tell no one for a month.' Hearing that the family's pig and poultry were also sickening she went to the stye and sprinkled some powder on the pig's back and in the poultry house. Pocketing 3 guineas she then informed the Hewitts that they had been 'overlooked' by a Mr. and Mrs. Slee.

At the trial the Slees appeared to say that they 'bore the Hewitts no ill-will but had done them repeated kindnesses.' Intriguingly William claimed that both his father and the pig were now healthy again - nevertheless the magistrates still fined Sarah £3 plus costs for 'telling fortunes. . . contrary to the Vagrancy Act of 1824.'

A few days later Sarah was again in court on the same charge only this time the complainant was P.c.Ridler an Exeter policeman. He had been sent undercover to obtain positive evidence of her fortune telling. Sarah again went through her cards routine adding that he was suffering from leg pain - which he was. On telling her that his baby was unwell she asked when it was born. He replied the 11th of November and she opened a bible at the 11th Psalm and told him to go home and read it with his wife. She also ordered him to 'place a lock of hair from behind the left ear of each member of your family in a bottle with a drop of water for three mornings following.' For this advice she charged him £2 2s with the promise that if he delivered the bottles to her she would prepare him some 'charms'. She then knelt before him, placed her hand on his left knee and said some words the policeman could not hear.

Asked if she had anything to say to this evidence Sarah spiritedly replied that she didn't ask for any money and turning to Ridler said 'Your knee is better and you walked out of my house better than you walked in.' She went on to claim that 'I can do a lot of good for a good many people.' She then rather spoilt her defence by claiming that the policeman was lying and that in fact he had only paid her 4/- in advance not the 5/- he told the court about and in any case hadn't been inside her house long enough for her to do all the things he claimed.

After listening to her rather contradictory denials for some time the magistrates hearing the case sentenced her to a month's hard labour in gaol as 'a rogue and vagabond.'

Further research has shown that Sarah had been in trouble before having been arrested on at least three occasions prior to this for being drunk and disorderly. On another occasion she untruthfully alleged that J.W.Cock of Appledore (where Sarah seems to have come from) was the father of her illegitimate child. I don't know what happened to Sarah after this 1901 trial but one would have expected her to foresee such problems and be able to avoid them if she actually did have any magical gifts! *North Devon Journal* 22.10.1998

11. A splendid worker in every department of public life

Every community has its 'Mr. (or Mrs.) Fix-it', the person who gets things done and on whom the community come to depend. When that person dies, of course, everyone suffers. In March 1910 Cecil Bevan of Lynmouth died aged just 45 and with his passing there went one of the most dynamic characters the town had ever seen.

He came from a family closely associated with the development of both Lynton and Lynmouth. His father William had been a builder who owned the Lyndale, Torrs and Lyn Valley

Hotels into which he had placed his sons Tom and Cecil as managers whilst he continued to build large houses in the local area.

Whilst not running his hotel Cecil Bevan spent most of his time undertaking aspects of public service or organising various local groups. He had been a member of the Lynton Urban District Council for 14 years being returned each time with a large majority. Although 'he deprecated the introduction of party politics into Council elections' he actually was 'a zealous Conservative' though it was noted that 'his every action as a councillor was actuated by an intense love for and pride in his native town.'

As well as serving on the council Cecil was Secretary to the local branch of the National Lifeboat Institution and served as Battery Quarter Master Sergeant in the area's Territorial artillery force. In this latter role he was also the 'energetic and assiduous President of the Territorial Recreation Committee.' Indeed his hotel was generally the venue for the annual regimental dinner.

When not on manoeuvres or in the council chamber Bevan was a keen Freemason, the harbourmaster at Lynmouth, the local agent for the Shipwrecked Mariners' Society and also the booking agent for Campbell and Company's steamer service!

Even with all these posts Bevan found time to follow his one hobby of sea fishing which he practiced from his boat the *Gannet* which, needless to say, he had built himself. His catches were apparently 'distributed with a lavish hand' amongst the poor of his home town. Photographs of the more impressive specimens were displayed in his hotel where they 'attracted the admiration and surprise of a long succession of visitors.'

At the inquest into his death the Coroner said his passing had touched him deeply as the dead man had been one of his best friends. Evidence came from a Dr.Warren who had warned Bevan to take life a little easier as he had a weak heart. The jury returned a verdict of death from natural causes.

The funeral was held a few days later when both Lynton and Lynmouth closed in mourning. All flags were at half-mast and all shops and schools were shut for the day. The funeral procession was headed by members of the local artillery company along with the Territorial band from Ilfracombe. They were followed by the local lifeboat crew 'wearing their life jackets', a large number of Freemasons, the local Boy Scout troop, the Coastguards, the Fire Brigade and the members of the Urban District Council. After a packed service the body was taken to the cemetery where three volleys were fired over the grave.

At a special council meeting a vote of condolence to Bevan's family was passed and the chairman reckoned 'they had lost one of their most useful members, a splendid worker in every department of public life.' How many people do we have like that today?

North Devon Journal 14.1.1999

12. The betting bankrupt of Lundy

I have written before about how Lundy became a bolthole for hard pushed debtors in the early nineteenth century and how bailiffs visited the island at their peril. As the century wore on, however, the island's owners introduced the rule of law and Lundy no longer provided a haven for the hunted. Just to show that old habits die hard, however, a story comes down to us from August 1910 when the *Journal* carried a long article headed 'Betting leads to failure - Bankrupt now living at Lundy Island.'

The gentleman in question was Arthur Charles Henry Stocks alias Arthur St.Claire who described himself as a farmer of Saunts Farm, Lundy Island. He had been tracked by his creditors to the island after two years of searching and after the authorities were informed was ordered to appear in Barnstaple before the local Registrar of Bankruptcy.

At his public examination the Registrar C.E.Chanter heard a bizarre story of recklessness and deception very alien to sedate North Devon. Stocks had begun life as a wheelwright and part-time farmer in Essex. He moved on to an 'art producing business' in London which did fairly well until a disastrous fire destroyed the underinsured premises and took much of his capital with it. Since February 1908 he had, in his own words, 'really not had any employment.'

Stocks had, in fact, taken to betting to try and make some easy money - with predictable results. Over one five month period

Stocks had placed bets with a Mr.Henckley which amounted to an incredible (for that time) £577 - with which he had only won £207. A little later in just the one month of May 1909 he lost £285. In his own words Stock 'got into a hole' and with the little money he had left travelled to Newmarket Races to try and win something 'but whatever I did went wrong.'

When asked if Henckley gave him time to pay his bills Stocks said no - rather 'He wrote me a very indignant letter.' Henckley then despatched a 'representative', presumably a strong arm man, to see Stocks and he took the unfortunate man's last £25.

Faced with disaster Stocks changed his name and disappeared. The Registrar asked 'was this flit to Lundy Island in connection at all with the affair with Mr.Henckley?' to which Stocks brazenly said 'No connection whatever.' He had been on Lundy for two years living in the Manor House which belonged to a Mr.Saunt. The owner had asked him to manage the island's hotel and 'if he could make it pay he was to get half the profits.' After a long period of refurbishment the hotel opened but 'there was no need for a balance sheet' as the gross takings over the first year's business were just £25 and over the second an even more meagre £10. On this basis Stocks 'was afraid there was no hope of profits for himself.'

The only money he did have was in a joint bank account with his sister who worked in Lundy's dairy. Unfortunately his sister was also keen on betting and needless to say 'Her account was a losing one'. Stocks' actual financial situation was that had £32 in the bank but faced claims of £584 of which some £340 were betting debts. Mr.Henckley as the main creditor was pressing for repayment and Stocks had no alternative but to be declared bankrupt. This the Registrar did whilst making strong comments about the stupidity of Stocks.

One wonders how many other desperate debtors read this and thought of disappearing to the island to escape their creditors - at least for the two years that Stocks had managed?
North Devon Journal 3.12.1998

13. Webber's Millions

Old fashioned folklore in the guise of belief in witches, black and white magic etc has withered over the last few years - only to be replaced by what is termed urban legends. These modern tales are often spun around half-truths or things we would like to be true but are not. Today they are often spread via the internet or tabloid newspapers as for example with the death of Princess Diana or the 9/11 conspiracy theories - but such beliefs can be traced back at least a century and one especially resonated with North Devonians.

In September 1924 the *Journal* published a small item headed 'The Webber Millions - Several North Devon Claimants.' The story was simple and as with all such tales is really rather vague as to details. Apparently 'Well over a century ago' a young man from Germansweek in North Devon called William Webber decided to try his luck in Australia. As the reporter put it with wonderful understatement, 'He had no particularly bright prospects, but unheard of luck came his way, and he discovered a gold mine' - as one does. This sounds as though it might just be possible but then if we are to believe the report he sold the mine and went to America where he invested his new wealth in real estate.

At this date New York was 'a comparatively small place, and Manhattan Island was little better than a swamp.' This land was cheap and Webber bought great chunks of it - and by 1924 this area was covered with skyscrapers - 'and the land is worth any price' including as it did most of Broadway!

At some point Webber married and had a daughter but when she grew up she chose a husband of whom William disapproved which caused the father to disinherit his daughter and leave his whole estate in limbo - to be distributed only after seven generations amongst his surviving descendants. By 1924 the value of this land was put at an eye-watering £115 million.

Needless to say there were at least 70 claimants - including a Mrs.Harry Guard of Higher Maudlin Street in Barnstaple. She had drawn up a family tree showing her descent from the Reverend Humphrey Webber, rector of Challacombe in 1665 -

which she claimed somehow linked her to William - a claim she backed up with numerous letters on the subject. Although Mrs.Guard was 69 'representatives' of her branch of the family were 'shortly to meet in London, and go thoroughly into the matter.'

Another claimant was a nephew of Bertha Perrin whose mother was a Webber from Germansweek. Bertha had been brought up at Chestwood House near Barnstaple and had 'many valuable papers bearing on the claim' but, sadly, these had been destroyed in a recent fire.

The *Journal* report ended by pointing out that the land had to go to somebody and 'the progress of the claims put forward by the North Devon aspirants to a 'share of the spoils' is therefore invested with an unusual degree of interest.' What a wonderful story!

I say story because there are a few glaring holes in the whole thing. I suspect William Webber was a real person and he did actually emigrate to Australia - but settlement of the continent only began in the late eighteenth century and no gold was discovered until the 'Gold Rush' of the 1850s. By that date New York was already a sizable city and the idea that one could just waltz in and buy great tracts of Manhattan Island is unlikely to say the least. Even more problematic is the seventh generation distribution idea. Generations are usually calculated at 25-30 years and even the lower figure gives a time span of some 175 years i.e. the start date of the will would date to around 1750 - some 20 years before Australia was even discovered by Captain Cook! I suspect the whole thing is spurious, albeit William Webber could have been a real person. A search of the internet reveals a very different story with one Wolfort Webber being the son of the Dutch King! Given that the Dutch did settle New York this seems a tale with a firmer, but still very shaky, foundation. Suffice to say no-one has ever claimed the Webber Millions be they North Devonian or Dutch - and that is the way it is going to stay.

14. Exotic Royalty at Hartland

It isn't often I write about things that are within living memory but this article is based on something that occurred some 60 years ago and may well be recalled by older North Devonians.

In August 1938 the *Journal* carried the astonishing headline, 'Emperor of Ethiopians at Hartland' with, below it 'Opens Church Fete'. Difficult as it is to believe today but Haile Selassie the Emperor of Ethiopia actually did come to Hartland to carry out this rather mundane duty.

The monarch who was then 46 years old had been crowned 'Negus' or king of his country in 1928 and two years later was created Emperor. Noted as a reforming leader he introduced many new ideas into his country to try and propel it into the twentieth century. Sadly his efforts were cut short when Mussolini, the fascist dictator of Italy, decided that he needed some African colonies to lend his dictatorship substance - and Ethiopia was a tempting prey.

An Italian army invaded in 1935 and although the Emperor lead the resistance bravely he was forced into exile in May 1936 and soon arrived in Britain. Here he spent five years travelling from one host to another not really knowing if he would ever see his country again.

As a Christian the Emperor was invited to various Church-sponsored functions and the fete at Hartland Abbey was one of these - thus the rather incongruous sight of an African Emperor whose followers claimed he descended from the Queen of Sheba standing in a field full of sideshows in North Devon.

The parish vicar, the Reverend Gregory, welcomed the royal visitor with a rousing speech saying, 'We greatly appreciate the generosity of your heart in coming to this remote corner of England to help forward the work of the Church of Christ in this place.' He added that everyone had been struck by the Emperor's 'wonderfully correct efforts to preserve the peace' and how, when war actually came, his 'bravery on the field of battle.' The clergyman finished his welcome with the statement that 'I will tell the people of Devonshire who are assembled that the gallant Ethiopians are still struggling against terrible odds to free their country from the aggressor' - although he didn't actually name Italy.

Haile Selassie's reply was given in Amharic and had to be translated as he went along which must have puzzled the Hartland parishioners. He denounced the invasion of his country pointing out that 'women are weeping, where is my husband; where is the father of my children; children are crying, where is my mother; where is my father?' The emotional charge behind these powerful rhetorical questions was rather wasted when he then added 'I would like finally to say that I hope you will all have an enjoyable time and I hope this bazaar which I have much pleasure in declaring open, will be a success.'

D.Stucley, the owner of Hartland Abbey, then made a short speech. Speaking himself as a soldier he had to admire the gallantry of the Emperor and his army 'against terrible odds'. These sentiments were seconded by W.J.Pillman.

The *Journal* report of this follows it with a rather bathetic list of stalls and stallholders such as 'Deck Quoits: J.Burrow', 'Rolling the Penny: Messrs L.Middle and L.Rowe' and 'Skittles: H.Prouse'.

When one considers that today Haile Selassie is revered as a God by the Rastafarians of Jamaica and Britain it seems even more amazing that he ever came to this rather isolated corner of North Devon.

North Devon Journal 15.4.1999

TOWN AND LANDSCAPE

15. Bideford Bridge Trust accounts

Accounts don't sound the most exciting of documents - but the older they get the more interesting they become. The Bideford Bridge Trust has probably been in existence since the bridge was built some 700 years ago. Over that time the trustees have created many documents though the earliest ones have long since disappeared. They do, however, still possess accounts from 1691 onwards and by looking at entries for just one year we can get a sense of the Trust's work.

The year 1734 was much like any other with its listings of rents coming in and payments going out. As one would expect many of the expenses were to do directly with the upkeep of the bridge. Thus we find George Dennis and two others being paid 5/6 (27.5p) 'to ffetch Mussells for the Bridge.' This doesn't refer to some sort of shellfish supper for the trustees but rather illustrates one of the odd ways in which the pillars of the bridge were protected from the scouring action of the River Torridge. The mussels were placed around the stone bases of the pillars and helped anchor the stones and mud in place. Indeed until well into the twentieth century the bridge carried a notice warning people not to remove the mussels under pain of court action!

A few months earlier in May Edward Jenkin was paid 17/2 (86p) for work 'ab[ou]t the Boat' whilst Robert Wren received the large sum of £3.0.5 (£3.02) 'for the Boat'. These entries refer to the 'Bridge Boat' that was used to allow maintenance to be carried out underneath the bridge arches at high tide.

Other bridge related outgoings were the 5/- (25p) paid to John Clouteman 'for sweeping the Bridge' - an ongoing necessity at this date when most traffic was horse-drawn. Another 1/6 (7.5p) went to an unnamed 'Stone Cutter' for supplying a 'Top Stone' - presumably a coping stone for the bridge's balustrade whilst 2/6 (12.5p) had to be spent in 'looking for the Cross of the Bridge w[he]n blown off.' This cross was a stone one set up half way across the bridge and seems to have been of some antiquity hence the money paid to find it.

Two payments are of some interest. Some £5.5.0 (£5.25) went to George Down 'ab[ou]t the Dialls' and a further £3.14.6 (£3.72.) went to John Marshall for 'painting the fface of the Diall At the Town Hall'. This refers to a sun dial that still exists on Bridge Buildings and was clearly important at this date before the erection of any public clocks in Bideford. Intriguingly 6d (2.5p) was paid to the Town Crier 'to forewarn people throwing Stones at the Dyall' - thus proving vandalism is nothing new!

Other sums were expended on repairs to the buildings owned by the Trust including 1/- (5p) to John Williams for 'a Stape key and mending the Lock for the Bogghowse' - whether this was a public toilet kept up at the Trust's expense or not is unrecorded.

One final group of payments merit comment. The Trustees' meetings were generally accompanied by alcohol - so that in May 4/6 (22.5p) was spent on 'Punch Ale Cyder etc & A Small Eating'. The trustees didn't just treat themselves, however, as at the annual public meeting re the Bridge accounts food and drink were provided for whoever came. Thus £5.10.8 (£5.54) was paid out for alcohol plus 'Tobacco & Candles'. Today's trustees don't get so much as a cup of coffee so things have changed somewhat - perhaps (and I write as a present day trustee) for the worse!

16. Eighteenth century council minutes

Council minutes may not be seen as the most exciting of documents but age lends interest to them. Barnstaple has a fine run of these going back a few hundred years and recently I examined one group from 1739-1754.

Many of the entries relate to instructions issued to bailiffs and rate collectors to ensure that their collections are up to date. Occasionally the entries give a fuller picture as in February 1739 when Joseph Short is ordered to pay the rents of his corporation owned house and shops under pain of having his goods seized by the Town Clerk. In the same entry 3 other people, Martha Babb, Robert Dennis and George Parminter are similarly warned.

The rest of the entries are very varied. Payments are made - such as the £10 'distributed by the Mayor and Aldermen to the most necessitous Poor' in Barnstaple owing to 'the very Severe Weather' in 1739. In January 1750 'the late great Storm' lead to £40 being laid out on repairs to the Long Bridge and the 'Crane and Boathouse' on Barnstaple Quay.

In September 1740 the Mayor is to 'proceed to ffinish the New Square by Levelling and Gravelling thereof' and providing drainage gutters. I assume this is the present-day Square at the end of the Bridge which was first created in 1715 - evidently the eighteenth century Barnstaple corporation moved rather slowly!

Two years later the corporation decided to 'repair the High Schooll' in St.Peter's churchyard and when the Bishop of Exeter visited the town in 1744 the Mayor was given permission to entertain him 'in such Handsome decent and Elegant manner' as he thought fit. This included providing a 'peece of Roast Beef' and 'a Kilderkin of Ale' for the town constables then on duty. The corporation was evidently exercised by the cost of entertaining as in 1749 it was noted that 'no Mayor shall be allowed any More than Three pounds for Muld wine' at the meeting to set the property rents.

One very odd entry dates from February 1743 when the corporation agreed to pay the legal costs of Matthew Rock, one of their members, who had been charged by Anthony Palmer with 'throwing away and Spoyling his Wigg'. This was on the odd basis that 'it Appeareing to us that what the said Mr.Rock did to the said Palmer was Justifiable.'

Of perhaps more importance was the entry 6 months earlier where it was noted that no new lease would be granted to the leaseholders of the 'Castle Meeting House' until they agreed 'not to permit any person to be Buryed there for the future.' Which non-conformist group this referred to is uncertain but it suggests that somewhere under the present day Cattle Market car park near the Castle is a forgotten cemetery.

On a happier note in 1739 the corporation recorded their thanks to Henry Rolle the Recorder of Barnstaple's magistrate's court for his gift of 'the Pictures of the Corporation.' As a nice return gesture they 'desire that the said Mr.Rolle that he will be pleased to Sit for his Picture at the Expense of the Corporation and that Mr.Mayor do the Same.' I believe these paintings are still to be seen in the Guildhall.

The oddest sounding entry to our ears comes in 1754 when it was ordered that any councillor who 'shall discover divulge or Disclose to any person or person whatsoever any Matter or Thing treated of or Debated in Council' was to be immediately removed from corporation membership. Today, of course, the *Journal* regularly reports council debates and we take this freedom for granted. Clearly our ancestors didn't have quite the same understanding of popular politics that we do today.

17. The Bridge Trust fire engine

The origins of the Bideford Bridge Trust are lost in the realms of history but over the 700 years or so it has been in being it has become the owner of large amounts of property the rents from which have been used for many charitable actions. As large property owners the Bridge trustees have been concerned with guarding against destructive fires.

This interest can be traced in the Trust's surviving minute books where the first reference occurs in December 1764 when the trustees decided to forego their annual dinner and put the money saved 'towards the subscription for the purchase of a good fire Engine for the good of the town.' A year later they agreed to spend £50 on 'a good fire Engine' provided that their fellow townspeople would 'Subscribe the remainder of the money.' Three years later in November 1768 they were still trying to get this cash but they must have anticipated success as the Steward (the Trust's secretary) was writing to the manufacturers to 'Inquire the price of the best constructed fire Engine' in September 1769.

Seven months after this the newly purchased engine was housed in 'the cellar' under the Town Hall (on the site of the present-day Bridge Buildings) which almost certainly wasn't underground but was a ground-floor storeroom. The Bridgewardens (the Trust's surveyors) were charged with taking it out once every two months 'to play off said Engine' and to erect shelves to hold 'the Leather pipes' which were the eighteenth century equivalent of our modern hoses. A later entry notes that the fire captain (Bideford's first) was George Heard.

By 1800 the feoffees were examining a second engine and in 1802 actually purchased one for £55. Costs were aided by an annual grant of 3 guineas from the Royal Exchange Assurance Office in London which presumably stemmed from their interest in stopping costly fires. At this date John Heard (possibly a relative of George) was paid 1 guinea to look after the engines. In 1805 Richard Cadd and Philip Tardrew were being paid 4 guineas to keep the engines 'in complete repair at their Expense.' The next year the two men raised their charges to £7 per annum which the trustees agreed to.

The presence of two fire engines, however, didn't prevent a 'dreadful Fire which happened last Tuesday Morning at Mr.William Carders, Potter, East the Water by which his Furse Ricks and some Houses adjoining were consumed and the whole of the Houses on that side of the Water were in imminent danger of being destroyed by fire.' As a result the trustees decided to write a clause into their leases that no potter was to keep more than a fortnight's worth of furse (used for firing the kilns) in any property rented from the Trust. The first potter to apply for a letting with this clause refused to accept it and so had his lease withheld until he saw the error of his ways six months later.

In 1812 the trustees must have decided that the town should help with costs as the minutes record that 'half the expence of the Fire Engines be paid by the Feoffees only.' Costs must have been minimal as it wasn't until 1829 that tenders were requested 'for supplying Leather Pipes for the two small Engines.' By 1836 there appears to have only been one engine and William Major was being paid £3.10.0 to look after it although in 1846 'the Bridge Engines' are referred to. The entry relating to this also notes that the West of England Insurance Company were being asked to provide new pipes for the engine 'in consideration of the extent of their Insurances in this Neighbourhood.' I wonder if modern insurance companies would contribute to the Devon Fire Service?

Regular maintenance was being carried out on the engine to keep it in good repair e.g. painting in 1838, overhauling in 1846, renewal of pipes and general repairs in 1846. The Minutes end in 1849 but the later story can be followed in Ian Arnold's *The Bideford Fire Brigade*' where the gradual change from a privately funded service to one we all support today is detailed.
North Devon Journal 24.6.1999

18. The birth of Barnstaple Pannier Market

The largest Victorian building in Barnstaple is the Pannier Market. Up until 1855, however, the market stalls had been erected in the High Street itself and the surrounding thoroughfares. This gave rise to many complaints about congestion and arguments between shopkeepers and the stallholders who pitched themselves outside the shops.

In the early years of the nineteenth century there was a move to provide a purpose-built market hall but nothing came of this - or of various other plans to fulfil this long felt want. It was not until 1851 that definite plans were drawn up to construct a weatherproof building to hold all those who wished to trade. The prime mover was the splendidly named councillor Cadwallader Palmer who had to battle against public indifference and political skulduggery before finally getting the market built in 1855.

Building operations cost nearly £6500 but the town council took out a loan to be repaid over 30 years so the ratepayers weren't unduly taxed. The architect was Robert D.Gould, the borough surveyor, and the builder was a Mr.Gribble.

The actual opening occurred in November 1855 when all the traders carried their panniers into the hall to be followed by large numbers of interested townspeople. The farmers' wives and daughters who actually did the trading had 'smiles that irradiated their countenances' which signified 'their gratification at their new location.' Vegetable and fruit sellers gathered at the High Street end whilst the Butchers Row side saw stalls selling tools, earthenware, boots and gloves. Butchers Row itself was also part of the development and had 35 'well ventilated' shop units. The Corn Market was where Queen's Hall now stands and had a Music Hall over it some 82' by 41'. The Pannier Market itself was completely asphalted which was reckoned to be more satisfactory than using wood or stone.

On its completion a celebration meal was given to the 'artisans' who had worked on it. Held in the Corn Market some 184 men sat down to the repast surrounded by banners bearing mottoes such as 'Our Queen and Country' and 'Success to the North Devon Railway'. Whilst this was going on a band played in the adjoining Market Hall to entertain the crowds who turned up to view the new building. One odd note was struck when 'with questionable taste' a 'number of ladies were introduced as spectators during the repast.' Clearly Barnstaple council were not very politically correct at this date!

The meal ended with a whole series of toasts being drunk - to the Queen, the clergy, Napoleon III (!), the architect, the builder and the labourers. The Reverend Henry Luxmoore, vicar of Barnstaple, reminded them 'that it was Saturday night, and not to allow the amusement of the evening to interfere with the more serious duties of the morrow.' A Captain Shearman, described as 'one of the Crimean heroes', returned thanks for the toast to the Army. William Avery, a councillor, also added that as a magistrate 'he could bear testimony to the uniform good conduct of the men' employed on the building. The very last toast on what must have been a fairly alcoholic evening was to Councillor Palmer who had actually been leaving the room when he heard his name being called. This toast was greeted with great cheering and conviviality.

The report in the *Journal* ends with a wonderful attack on those who had tried to stop the Market going ahead, 'the small men who have from the commencement opposed the market scheme, had sufficient discretion to absent themselves, or to hide their diminished heads.'

With its 150th anniversary soon approaching should the present-day council not start planning another celebratory meal in the Market - perhaps using food from the market itself to provide a repast' for today's schoolchildren?

North Devon Journal 16.12.1999

19. A dispute over the Bideford paint mines

Up until the 1960s culm or anthracite, a form of coal, was mined in Bideford, the material being used in a variety of ways but notably to make a richly pigmented black paint. Records of this activity are, however, scarce. In July 1856 a case was heard at the County Court in Bideford Town Hall that sheds some light on the trade.

William Mill a local watchmaker of East-the-Water was claiming £50 damages from the Bideford Anthracite Mining Company on three grounds - his land had been undermined, his well had dried up and an aerial tramway had been erected next to his property which scattered dust over his house.

William gave evidence as to being the owner of a house and malthouse which had been in his family for about 160 years. Some 12 years before the Company had begun mining operations nearby. Since then a well which served the malthouse had completely dried up and a wall erected only a few years previously had cracked in five places. The dust from the tramway had driven off one of Mill's tenants and he could now only let the property at a reduced rent. He had complained to the Company and hired an independent expert to inspect the mine workings but the Company refused to allow him access - hence the court case.

His main witness was a Mr.Pollard who had actually owned and worked the mine for 20 years before selling it in 1846 to the Company. He had then taken the tenancy of Mill's house and supported all that his landlord had said and as an expert his evidence carried a lot of weight so that the case looked very strong.

A neighbour James Vickery then gave evidence as to cracks in his walls adding 'we never had black dust in our houses before the tramway was erected. It is a great injury.' A gardener John Cawsey then recounted how he had been planting broccoli in the garden of Mill's house when 'the ground gave way with me' about a foot.

The Company's lawyer then began his case by saying that 'The Company were ever ready to make reasonable compensation for any injuries where they were fairly liable.' In this case, however, they were not responsible. They denied outright that their shafts went under Mill's property - indeed they missed it by some nine feet.

Captain Skews (the title seems to have been honorific), a professional miner, gave evidence as to the mine having been worked for some 300 years and in that time no shafts had ever gone underneath Mill's property or land. He had proved this by 'dialling' i.e. locating his exact position underground by a form of trigonometry. As the shaft was 180 feet deep he couldn't see how garden soil could sink so very far above, indeed 'it was ridiculous'. He had inspected the cracks in the walls and reckoned that 'a thick coat of whitewash will fill them.'

As to the dust from the tramway he lived underneath its course from the mine to the quayside and he 'experienced no nuisance from it.' In fact the culm was brought to the surface by a 'water balance' (something like the mechanism still used today for the Lynton Cliff Railway) and water from this wetted the culm on its way up the shaft to such an extent that there was no dust. He added that all his drinking water was collected from the run-off from the roof of his house - and he never found it polluted. His neighbours reckoned it to be 'beautiful water'.

Evidence was then offered that Mill had demanded that the Company buy his house for £300 - which the directors considered a large over-valuation. It was suggested that Mill had only brought the case to court in a fit of pique and in an attempt to pressurise the Company to purchase a property they had no use for.

Faced with two completely different sets of claims the judge adjourned the case to go and inspect the wall, dry well and garden himself. Returning to the Town Hall he gave it as his opinion that the wall had only experienced natural slippage down the hill whilst the drying of the well was nothing to do with the mine. The dust was a difficult feature but he didn't think it a major problem - and so only awarded Mill sixpence in damages with no costs.

So ended the case doubtless to Mill's chagrin. The tramway survived another nine years and can be seen on old photographs of the area. Very little remains today to remind Bidefordians of a once major industry in their town.

North Devon Journal 13.5.1999

20. The building of Holsworthy Market

Holsworthy market stands at the heart of the town as it has done for the last 140 years. Previous to this it had stood in Higher Square being built on 'low brick columns' but had gradually deteriorated. In the 1840s a group of leading townsmen decided that a new one was needed. Over a long period of time they met 'much difficulty and discouragement' but being determined they eventually succeeded and on August 11th 1857 they celebrated the laying of the foundation stone of the new market on a site previously occupied by an old school and the stables of the Stanhope Arms.

The *Journal* carried a long report on this event explaining that 'the formal laying of the first stone of a new market created no little excitement' - so much so that the town 'became the scene of a greater amount of gaiety and rejoicing than has been witnessed in it for many a day.' All the town's shopkeepers closed at 1 p.m. and a huge crowd collected in the Square.

Here they would have seen every shop and house decorated with 'floral and arborescent decorations'. There were 'green bowers' and 'triumphal arches' including one which stretched across Union Street which was surmounted with a huge Union Jack flag. Banners were also erected across the roads leading to the Square bearing mottoes such as 'Success to Agriculture', 'Trade and Commerce', 'Hearts of Oak' and even the wordy 'Welcome to the Rev.J.C.D.Yule, the Founder of the Market'. This gentleman had acted as Secretary to the group behind the new market building. Over the post office was a huge floral 'VR' in honour of the Queen.

The most commonly celebrated name on the banners, however, was that of Miss Jane Meyrick and her two sisters who were notable local philanthropists who had 'materially assisted in providing the means for the erection of the building'. There were banners reading 'Meyrick, a name dear to all', 'Welcome kind and noble lady' and 'The Ladies at Bodmeyrick, God bless them'.

At 2 p.m. a massive procession formed up in the Square headed by the Hatherleigh Town Band. They were followed by Mr.Willis the architect, the contractors and their 'Artificers, in their working dress, carrying their tools'. Then came the committee of townsmen, '20 Ladies, who were to preside at the tea tables' and two of the Meyrick sisters accompanied by the local clergy. These notables headed three hundred of 'The Gentry and Tradesmen of the Town and Neighbourhood', the whole being completed by three hundred local schoolchildren and their teachers.

The procession set off from Bodmeyrick House going through North, Union, Bodmin and Wellington Streets to the Higher Square with girls 'strewing flowers' before the Meyrick sisters. Here Jane Meyrick was presented with a silver trowel and salver which she used to spread some mortar onto which the inscribed foundation stone was 'lowered to its bed by machinery'. This was met with 'loud and repeated cheering'. The Rev.Yule then called for three cheers for the Queen, Earl Stanhope (the lord of the manor) and the Meyrick sisters - the cheers were 'deafening' and 'tears rolled over many a cheek from the impulses of grateful and affectionate emotion.' Following the National Anthem the procession formed up again and moved off to take tea.

Tables had been set out in the Square where 3000 cakes and tea were provided for all. At the completion of this the 'venerable rector of the parish the Rev.Roger Kingdon' presented a piece of silver plate to the Meyrick sisters which Jane said 'will be held sacred by us, and transmitted to each branch of our family as long as one remains to receive it.'

The rest of the day saw the children playing games at King's Wood whilst their parents were entertained by the band and the Holsworthy Glee Club. At dusk the National Anthem was played to mark the finale to this exciting day which doubtless stayed in peoples' memories for many a year afterwards.
North Devon Journal 3.6.1999

21. A new school in Barnstaple

The magnificent building at the corner of the Strand and Cross Street in Barnstaple today houses a building society on its groundfloor with a martial arts academy above it. Odd uses for what started life as a Congregational Church school in 1894.

Its opening ceremony on April 4 of that year was decidedly low-key but was reported at length in the *Journal*. The article began with a history of Congregationalism in the town which went back to 1662. As well as being the earliest nonconformist sect in Barnstaple they were also the first to open a Sunday School - as long ago as 1805. In 1859 they erected a school on the Strand/Cross Street corner which up until then had been the site of a notorious building known as Rats Castle.

The school was very successful and the chapel leaders looked to enlarge the building but discovered this was not possible and so complete demolition and rebuilding was decided on. To enlarge the site the sect purchased an adjoining house in Cross Street and demolished it.

The architect chosen to design the building was Lindley Bridgman whose work was described as 'a handsome structure, lofty and admirably proportioned.' Designed in the Gothic style the building had 'a commodious Lecture Hall' on the ground floor which 'although large, has a pleasant cheery appearance.' The main hall contained a rostrum and moveable railings to extend the platform if needed. 'Handsome' gas brackets supplied artificial light and the whole was heated by a large fireplace. The heavily-carved porchway with its mosaic floor and painted glass was described at length but this has long gone.

The entrance at the back led, via fireproof stairs, to the schoolrooms on the upper floors. On the first floor there were nine classrooms to hold 240 scholars whilst the second floor had the same number of classrooms but giving space for 242 children. If completely filled nearly 1000 people could be accommodated so it is good to know that 'Ventilation and sanitation are throughout on the most approved principles.'

The handrail up the stairs was 'massive and handsome' though it was noted that 'knobs' were 'inserted at intervals to prevent the possibility of lads incurring the risk of sliding on it.' A further large room was available at the top of the building whilst in the basement was a kitchen and storeroom which had a trapdoor to connect it with the main hall 'so that tea requisites can be obtained without a journey to the basement,' which sounds surprisingly modern.

The opening ceremony itself in the afternoon was conducted by the Reverend Mr.Rutty who merely unlocked the main door, led in a small party of church members and held a short service. The Sunday School children were then served a celebration tea by their teachers whilst their parents had a similar meal in the main hall.

A large meeting in the evening heard a series of speakers praise the builders and those whose efforts had raised the necessary money. One commented that 'The best organisations of England all sprang out of the Sunday Schools' although what this actually meant is unclear. A large number of congratulatory messages from sister churches and schools were then read out and thus ended the first day in use of the building although it was noted that its full cost had still to be raised and so a 'grand Bazaar' was to be held to help clear the debt. Today the building is greatly altered inside but apart from its ground floor frontage its exterior is still as it was on the day it opened just over a century ago. *North Devon Journal* 1.1.2001

22. Heroic efforts to reclaim marshland on the Taw estuary
Farming during the nineteenth century was a lively industry with new inventions designed to make the job easier and profitable coming along regularly. The new ideas were often discussed in some depth in the pages of the *Journal* and among these was a series of three published in 1861 penned by Nicholas Whitley, who described himself as a 'Surveyor' of Truro.

One piece was titled 'On the embankment and reclaiming of the marshlands of the manor of Heanton Punchardon.' He began by noting that the first attempt to reclaim this area of sand, mud and clay came when a Mr.Green of Exeter was appointed to build a 'substantial embankment' two miles long which enclosed some 600 acres for cultivation. Local observers noted that a short embankment across Braunton Pill would have reclaimed an even larger area. Mr.Green apparently urged the adoption of this plan but was instructed to do otherwise.

The main embankment he built was successful but enclosure remained incomplete until the early 1850s when William Williams purchased the local manor and commissioned Whitley to report on reclaiming the remainder. The report was not very encouraging in that six miles of bank would have to be built to reclaim 400 acres. Some three-quarters of a mile of this, across Broadsand, would have to be 18 feet high 'over a quicksand where no solid ground could be touched with a 20 foot boring rod.'

Nothing daunted Mr. Williams asked for detailed plans. His first problem was deciding on what form the embankment should take - and for his inspiration he turned to the pebble ridge at Westward Ho! After taking a careful cross-section of the natural ridge Whitley began constructing his embankment and had the satisfaction of noting that 'during the heavy gales which in the past year have destroyed much seaside works, not a yard of paving has been moved on these embankments.'

The bank was constructed using earth coated with a three foot deep layer of puddle or saturated clay. Stones were placed on the slope to a depth of nine inches which was increased to a foot on exposed areas. Where the bank rested on just sand the clay coating was extended three feet deep into the river bed to prevent undercutting. The stone used was slate from the Braunton Down quarry supplemented with a few 'egg shaped boulders' from Crow Point.

The first area to be enclosed was Chivenor Marsh, the work being carried on to Wrafton Marshes where a channel some 1200 foot long, 90 feet wide and 16 feet deep had to be cut for the new outlet of the Pill. Then, Horsey Island was circled but the scouring action of the Taw meant faggots of furze had to be used to hold the sand in place.

Whitley notes that closing the final gap on 15 June 1857 saw 320 men operating 140 carts 'three abreast' bringing material to the site between the tides. Over just three hours they managed to raise a six foot high embankment - and thus complete the reclamation of 200 acres of marshland. The overall cost was £18,000. Whitley calculated the land was returning £1000 a year - not a bad rate for the time.

Horsey Island and the new 'cut' still exist but much of the land reclaimed by Whitley is now under the tarmac of the Chivenor base - one wonders what the proud Victorian surveyor would have made of this alteration?

North Devon Journal 29.3.2001

23. Swimbridge en fete

In March 1863 the Prince of Wales, later King Edward VII, married Princess Alexandra of Denmark. Needless to say the nation was convulsed in patriotic celebrations and North Devon rejoiced along with everywhere else. Naturally the *Journal* covered these in great details though most were similar in scope and size. The village of Swimbridge stands out, however, for the effort put in by the inhabitants to make it a real red-letter day. Indeed the *Journal* report reckoned the village and villagers 'were of opinion it not only had never seen the like before but it would never see the like again.'

J.G.Maxwell the village squire had supplied anyone who asked with 'an unlimited supply of magnificent evergreens' which were used to build 'triumphant arches within and without, over public paths and private ways'. Attached to these were hundreds of red, white and blue rosettes. These were all in place early on the day which began with the church bells being rung at length.

The actual celebrations began at 3 p.m. when 200 'tradesmen and labourers' sat down to a meal in a room provided by John Smyth the village churchwarden and owner of a large tannery. This room too was festooned with evergreen branches, mottoes and English and Danish flags. Grace was said by the Reverend John Russell and then everyone ate until 'all the guests had expressed their conviction that nature could do no more.'

Following the meal a whole string of toasts were drunk - lead off with ones to 'The Queen' and 'The Bride and Bridegroom'.

This latter was given by Russell who reckoned 'The match was one of affection and there was every prospect of happiness for the Royal pair' - a hope that sadly was not to be fulfilled. He went on to next toast the organising committee adding that 'he hoped all would go home soberly and peaceably - not making it an occasion for debauchery'. J.G.Maxwell responded saying 'he was confident in the men - only afraid of the women' - which was greeted with 'Roars of laughter'. The final toast was to the Reverend Mr.Russell and 'Again and again rose cheer upon cheer till lungs were well nigh exhausted.'

Whilst the men were dining some 200 women were drinking tea in the School room and 300 children were gathered in a field behind the church. Here they played games such as climbing the greasy pole and racing in sacks. The sports ended with the singing of the National Anthem which included a special verse. This went as follows:

Hear, Lord, a nation's prayer,
The Prince and Bride long spare,
To cheer the Queen,
When at some future day
Albert this isle shall sway,
Lord grant us that he may
Rule like our Queen
(Albert was Edward's first name.)

The organising committee then had a meal at the Lamb and Flag Inn before moving on to a ball at 9 p.m. held in the school-room. Here dancing was 'kept up till a late, or rather, an early hour' with only a break to view a monster celebration bonfire on Codden Hill which could be seen clearly for miles. So ended a day to be remembered with some 700 inhabitants of Swimbridge gathered to celebrate a Royal event - will we see the like if Harry or William ever marries I wonder?
North Devon Journal 14.8.2003

24. Fern Crazy

For some decades in the middle of the nineteenth century fern collecting was a national obsession. People would scour the hills and valleys of Britain for different species, press a frond or two between sheets of paper and mount them in large scrap books. This obsession was mirrored in the creation of furniture and knick-knacks based around the distinctive appearance of these lowly specimens of vegetation.

Devon, with its wet climate, was home to a wide range of ferns and not surprisingly, became one of the main centres of the craze - indeed it could be said that here in the north of the county fern collecting had as big an effect on the local tourist industry as did Charles Kingsley's book '*Westward Ho!*'

In January 1865 the *Journal* published the travel diary of a group of 'Fern Hunters' who apparently set out from the Midlands in July 1864 to see what they could find in North Devon to add to their collections. The writer remains anonymous but he stressed that his companions were of the 'right sort' in that they weren't averse to 'do a little climbing when there is some risk' and weren't afraid of getting wet in the search for specimens.

The group came by train to Bristol and there caught the *Princess Royal* steamer for Ilfracombe. Unfortunately the Bristol Channel was very rough and they were all sea-sick before arriving in the North Devon resort some 8 hours later. The party were much taken with the town which was 'a pretty place, a nice place, an agreeable place, a gay place' - how words change their meaning! Promenading and attending balls were the main attraction along with 'tunnels cut through the hills to reach the beach which would otherwise be inaccessible except at low water.' Additionally tourists could ride 'shaggy donkeys looking as if they were fed on one straw per day.'

The writer notes that as a port Ilfracombe had 'gradually declined, and it is now not heard of except as a watering place' - though it was the 'headquarters of North Devonshire fern hunters.' The group tried to get rooms at 'the principal inns' but as all were fully booked they were reduced to staying in an unnamed hotel 'of considerable pretensions but of very moderate capacity.' If we are to believe the author this lack of rooms was due to the huge number of fern hunters who were staying in the resort - which perhaps gives some idea of how popular the hobby was at this date.

Indeed so widespread was it that there were at least two professional fern hunters who could be hired by amateurs to help locate the rarer specimens. These men are named as Moule and Dadds both of whom 'professed to have left but few stones unturned within a circuit of some dozen miles of Ilfracombe.'

The party hired Dadds who took them on an outing to Combe Martin and helped them locate some rare specimens on trees and walls on the route. At Berrynarbor some 'wet banks' yielded up more exciting varieties - as did Combe Martin itself where they stayed the night. Unfortunately they were not impressed with the village noting that it 'is a little short of charming, truth to speak, it looks best at a distance.'

The next day they pushed on to Lynton having hired the only carriage in the village - which was pulled by a very 'sorry' horse. As they left they paused under a 'festoon strung across the village street, made in great part of ferns.' To fern collectors, of course, this was very exciting and, after making enquiries, they found it marked the celebration of a marriage and had been made by the pupils of the local Sunday School.

Part way along to Lynton most of the party alighted from the carriage to hunt ferns leaving the driver and one member to travel on to the Miller's Arms. After a successful fern 'foray' they walked on to the inn - only to find no-one there. Their approach to the place was itself rather hazardous as someone 'had put two hives of bees right in the middle of the path leading to the inn door!' The inn itself was 'one of the most primitive "publics" chance has ever thrown us into.' The room was only 10ft square and was crowded with 'all kinds of little prints, pictures and antique crockery.' Unfortunately when the group asked for a glass of whiskey each the landlady had to explain that she didn't have much in stock as they were limited to a quart at a time. The thirsty fern hunters therefore satisfied themselves with cider, clotted cream - 'a local dainty', bread, butter and cheese.

Whilst they were eating they chatted to the landlord who they found had a bewildering number of jobs. Not only was he the innkeeper but he also ran the local mill, was the village church-warden and Overseer of the Poor, Surveyor of the Highways, Collector of Rates and Taxes - and a farmer! Truly a man of many parts.

From here the party passed on to Hunter's Inn and out of history - but we must be glad that at least one Victorian 'fern hunter' left this account as a memoir of what was a huge craze. Perhaps the local Tourist Boards could look into reviving this lost hobby in order to attract new tourists back into North Devon'

25. Bone Hill in Northam
For many of the smaller features of our villages it is hard, if not impossible, to discover their history - the story of wells, open spaces and bus stops amongst others rarely feature in documents yet they add much to the landscape and would be sorely missed if they were not there. One such site is in Northam. Known as Bone Hill the area today houses a tall flagpole, a series of stones bearing carvings recording the names of British heroes, a few seats - and some disused toilets. When it was set up, however, it was very different.

The story begins on December 6 1866 when a parish meeting was held in Northam and a committee established 'to raise subscriptions and carry out the improvement of Bone Hill.' The members must have been fairly dynamic as within 5 months they were reporting back on the completion of their work.

The report began 'The desire of the Committee has been simply this; to form a pleasant Village Green and Playground, and make it easy of access on every side.' To meet this aim they formed four openings at the 'four corners of the hill'. Across the top of the hill a path was constructed to allow locals to continue their long time custom of collecting water 'from the Holy well.'

On the seaward facing side they had erected nine benches 'of green heart timber, varnished' plus 'a large garden chair, painted green.' The top of the hill, about half of the area, had been levelled and grassed and gravelled over. Committee members had considered planting the other half with 'flowering shrubs and evergreens' but thought children would inevitably damage any such plants - so merely planted a thorn fence. The whole area had been enclosed by a dry stone wall topped with oval stones from the Westward Ho! pebble ridge. Two gate pillars and a gate had also been erected - which took the expenditure over the budget.

The money for the work plus the raw materials came from over 100 subscribers. The work had been deliberately carried out in January 'during the snow storms' to provide work for local men who were otherwise unemployed. The only failure the committee reported was that they did not have enough money to build a 'Look-out House' or Summer House on the hill. This was to have been stone built, octagonal in form and some 13' in diameter with a cost estimated at just £18. The committee noted that 'they would happily receive any subscriptions to build this and thus complete the scheme.'

The report ended rather oddly by pointing out that due to the work 'the youth of Northam have been deprived of their favourite pastime' of standing up bottles, old pans and tin kettles on the hill and smashing them by throwing stones. Apparently these bottles 'were constantly being deposited on the hill' which suggests Bone Hill was viewed as a rubbish dump before these improvements. The committee expressed the hope that the 'rising generation of Northam' would now 'betake themselves to sports which may prove equally agreeable to themselves and be at the same time less dangers to horses' and pedestrians than before.

The report closed with some accounts which show that the total expenditure was £51.7.4 (£51.37) which seems remarkably cheap. Most of the work was carried out by John Cann and the two 'principal promoters of the improvement' were given as Thomas Pynsent and J.B.Gordon. Today Bone Hill is still a pleasant spot though there have been discussions over its future - whatever that holds it is nice to know about its past.

North Devon Journal 18.11.2005

26. A deadly house at Burrington

With the surge in house prices over the last decade dilapidated buildings have virtually disappeared through the attentions of developers and keen amateurs. Not only has this improved the look of our villages and towns but it has also made places safer - something that one family in Burrington in 1870 would have appreciated.

One Saturday afternoon in January at Penniford near Burrington the chimney on one of a pair of semi-detached cottages collapsed without warning. As a result 3 people died - William Gould aged 91 and two girls named Bird aged 11 and 9. At the inquest some terrible evidence came out.

After viewing the three bodies the inquest jury began listening to various witnesses. The first was Mary Bird wife of a Burrington labourer and mother of the two dead girls. She began by saying the cottage had been leased to Mr.Buckingham, a solicitor of Exeter, from the Earl of Portsmouth. Her husband had moved into the cottage with her and their four children along with William Gould who was her father-in-law.

On the Friday before the disaster the whole household with the exception of her husband who was working in Barnstaple went to bed at 9 p.m. Mary didn't sleep well, however, as one of her children was ill and she had to get up to attend to them. Around midnight she was up and the old man William who had woken up began chatting to her about the child's illness. Whilst they were talking they 'heard something littering down' - which she dismissed as 'only the plaster'. She did though try to get a light to see what was happening more clearly, but in her own chilling words, 'Whilst I was feeling for one the house came tumbling down all around us.' She went on to explain that she too would have died in the rubble had it not been for the bravery of her neighbour Thomas Hill who rushed to rescue her. Two of her children, Eliza and William, escaped and were only 'bruised a little' but of the other two she could only say 'I never heard a voice or a sound.'

The coroner conducting the inquest then asked her if she had ever complained about the state of the cottage? She said yes especially the dampness of the house adding 'I was wearying of living in the house, and wanted to get away from there.' She added that on the Saturday evening as she was putting one daughter to bed the girl had said 'I am afraid to live here look at those cracks.' Thinking they were only surface cracks she comforted her child and went to bed herself.

At this point the landlord Buckingham butted in and rather bizarrely seemed to suggest that having Gould in the house somehow strained the floor and led to the building's collapse. Following this interruption Thomas Hill appeared to give his evidence. He was Mary's brother-in-law as well as her neighbour and simply recounted his story as to dragging the survivors out though he did add 'Mr.Buckingham has been a kind landlord to me' but rather spoilt the effect by adding 'My cottage is in a bad state'. P.c.Blackmore followed Hill describing in horribly graphic detail the positions of and injuries to the bodies

A local mason John Ford then gave his account. He had actually inspected the cottage on the Friday but said 'I didn't see any danger there' though he said the fact that the stone chimney stack rested on a wet cob wall was asking for trouble.

The final person called was the landlord Buckingham who claimed to have hired Ford to inspect the cottage and carry out any necessary repairs. Oddly these seemed to be confined to the roof. On being cross-examined by the jury foreman Buckingham became very uncomfortable and quickly decided that attack was his best form of defence as he turned on the foreman saying 'I think you are a very unfit man to be in the place you are. The way in which you have put questions is most improper. You are taking a very one sided view of the matter.'

The coroner stepped in to calm him down and after summing up the evidence the jury 'after some little consideration' returned their verdict 'We believe the deaths of these persons to be accidental, through the fall of a house, which, however, at the time was out of repair.' They then presented their fees to Mary Bird - no mention you will notice of compensation for the family or condemnation of Buckingham. As I stated at the beginning of this article thank goodness such dangerous states of dereliction are rare today.

27. The very landed gentry

There has been much news lately of the BBC-inspired 'Computer Domesday Project' - a joint effort by hundreds of schools throughout the country to record on computer disc a view of our present-day life in Britain. It has been hailed as a 'second Domesday' but in actual fact it should be termed a 'third Domesday'.

The first occurred in 1086 when William the Conqueror decided to catalogue what he had captured whilst the second dates from 1872-3 and is rather prosaically entitled 'Return of Owners of land in England and Wales exclusive of the Metropolis.' The original survey in 1086 was for tax purposes but this Victorian one originated out of class politics.

In February 1872 there was a question in Parliament about the census of the previous year which had as its ultimate aim the scotching of rumours surrounding the very small number of landowners shown in that census. An M.P. referred to 'the extraordinary statements made in certain newspapers and at some public meetings, respecting the wonderfully small numbers of landed proprietors in this country.'

He had added, 'The fact was that very few persons were returned in the census under the designation of "owners of land".' This lack of numbers was taken to show that the 'landed gentry' were extremely well-landed indeed and that the greater part of Britain was in fact owned by very few people.

Parliament ordered a comprehensive survey to be taken to show, in the words of the eventual report:

'The number and names of owners of land of one acre upwards, whether built upon or not, in each county with estimated acreages and annual gross estimated rental of the property belonging to each owner.'
'The number of owners of land, whether built upon or not of less than one acre, with the estimated aggregate acreage and the aggregate gross estimated rental of the land of such owners.'
'The estimated extent of commons and waste lands in each county.'

The finished report for Devon showed 21,647 landowners with less than one acre and 10,162 with more than one acre. Owners are listed alphabetically and thus provide a quick reference for present day family historians. The actual details of landholdings in the list are of interest even today. The great landowners are obvious - Earl Fortescue owned 20,171 acres whilst the Duke of Bedford owned 22,607 acres. Both, however, were eclipsed by the Hon.Mark Rolle of Stevenstone House in St.Giles near Torrington who owned a grand total of 45,088 acres.

Amongst the smaller owners were William Adams of Fremington with his 29 acres, William Bale senior of Braunton with 71 acres and Joshua Avery of Ilfracombe with 22 acres. Some land was held by charitable bodies - thus the trustees of the Andrew Dole in Bideford owned just two acres. Interestingly they still own this land though now it is permanently leased to Bideford College to provide a playing field.

The overall results, in Devon at least, seem to show that the 'landed gentry' were indeed very 'landed' - possibly not quite the outcome that the M.P's. had in mind when they commissioned the report. One wonders what a similar survey would reveal today?

North Devon Journal-Herald 5.6.1986

28. Living by the rule book

In 1879 a firm of local printers produced a small booklet with a long title - *'Byelaws made by the Town Council of the Borough of Bideford acting as the Urban Sanitary Authority Allowed by the Local Government Board.'* Admittedly such things as old municipal byelaws don't sound very interesting but reading them does illustrate the lives of our Victorian ancestors in some surprising ways.

The booklet begins with those rules covering the cleanliness of the town. The first should give us pause for thought today as we complain about the litter in our streets as it orders that every property owner must 'once at least in every day, Sundays excepted, cleanse the footways and pavements' in front of their premises. Some of our shopping centres, fouled as they are by dogs, could do with this treatment today.

Another byelaw in the same section orders that all property owners should 'once at least in every three months, cleanse every earth closet belonging to their premises.' This is an odoriferous reminder that flushing toilets were uncommon at this date. The material so produced by this cleaning was collected, in a covered cart, by the euphemistically named 'night soil men' who sold it on to farmers as manure. Not the most hygienic thing to do with raw human sewage perhaps but certainly very environmentally acceptable (and after all South West Water are doing the same thing with the new sewage works at Cornborough.)

In addition to this rule ashpits had to be cleaned at least once a week, a necessity in the days when open fires supplied all hot water and provided the only cooking facilities available for most people. Anyone who flouted any of these byelaws was laying themselves open to a fine of £2.

In the booklet there then followed a whole series of byelaws concerning the keeping of animals. No pigs or cattle were to be kept within fifty feet of any house in the town and all animal dung had to be kept away from sources of human drinking water and even the times the dung could be removed during the day were strictly controlled.

A further collection of rules governed *Common Lodging Houses* beginning with maximum possible numbers of lodgers - and a stern order concerning the separation of the sexes. Windows in all rooms had to be opened for at least two hours a day for airing purposes (unless the weather was too bad!) As soon as lodgers departed their bedding had to be aired for at least an hour - but there was no rule specifying that it had to be washed! All illnesses of lodgers had to be reported to the Council's Medical Officer of Health. Landlords were ordered not to use kitchens as bedrooms and to display a complete set of byelaws in their lodging house where guests could see them. Any offences against these rules, and there were twenty six altogether, rendered the landlord open to an initial fine of £2 with an additional fine of 50p per day for as long as the offences continued.

The booklet also contains rules relating to building standards and slaughter- houses but these are for the most part more technical and less interesting perhaps than the ones already discussed. Nowadays there are far fewer local byelaws most councils merely acting as agents for centrally imposed rules and regulations - another example of the loss of local democracy apparent all through this century.
North Devon Journal 25.2.1999

29. A 'Leicestershire Lady' writes of Lundy

In the nineteenth century the *Journal* editor often reprinted articles from other newspapers if he thought his readers would be interested in them. In 1886 he reproduced 'The Adventures of a Visit to and Scenes on Lundy Island' by 'A Leicestershire Lady' from an unnamed paper of that county. I am unsure who the writer was although she talks of the lessee of the island, T.H.Wright, being her cousin.

Arriving with a female companion at Ilfracombe she stayed in the Royal Britannia Hotel but the weather was too rough for Captain Reid of the *Velindra*, which visited the island once a week, to attempt a crossing. Thwarted the women travelled to Instow and the next day set off at 7 a.m. in the *Gannet* sailed by Captain Dark.

Unfortunately a sharp current caused the boat to run into a ship at anchor in the estuary and Dark had to shout out 'All lie down flat on deck' in order to avoid the other ship's bowsprit mast as it swept across them. Worse was to come. As their boat crossed the Bideford Bar it 'shipped water rather freely' and the passengers were drenched. So bad did it get that Dark decided to return to port. Not an auspicious start but the sea hasn't always been kind to those seeking to get to Lundy.

His two passengers along with six others had to wait another 2 days until the 10th. September before setting off again, the crossing taking some 3$\frac{1}{4}$ hours. Arriving at the Lundy anchorage they found several sailing craft and steamers already present. The writer records the fact that at times more than a hundred craft were anchored there.

Coming ashore they were taken up from the beach by a carriage belonging to Miss Heaven a member of the family who owned the island. Whilst on Lundy they stayed at 'The Lone Ranche' cottage which had a 'grand' view over the sea and cliffs. Once unpacked they began to explore the island.

Their first stop was the 'pretty little iron church' erected by the Heaven family. This was a prefabricated affair which nonetheless could seat 100 people. It was to be another 10 years before the present church of St.Helen's was begun.

They then recorded the agricultural activity they observed. Oats, turnips, barley and swedes were grown and 100 cattle and 1200 sheep raised. These latter were sold either to passing ships or in the markets on the mainland. At that time an apparently experimental crop of rape was being tried which had grown to a height of over 7 feet. The writer suggests that Lundy could provide a useful training for 'young men wishing to prepare for Colonial farming' as the lessee was 'an old Colonist' himself who used techniques picked up whilst farming in Australia, New Zealand and South America.

Travelling around the island they came across a 'series of chasms' running parallel to the cliff edge which reached up to 20' wide and 80' in depth. These, so it was claimed, appeared in 1755 at the same time as the massive earthquake which destroyed Lisbon in Portugal. However they were formed the chasms were full of ferns which were greatly prized by Victorian collectors who dried and mounted them in large albums.

Reaching the lighthouse they climbed all 127 steps reckoning the view from the top 'well repays the fatigue' experienced. A walk to Marisco Castle followed but isn't described as the writer herself admitted 'I feel myself quite inadequate to attempt to do justice to any account worthy of an old ruin fraught with such graphic and daring annals of loyalty, rebellion, romance, brigandage, piracy and bloodshed.' So ended their first day on Lundy.

Getting up the next morning they were confined to their cottage for a few hours until a heavy mist lifted. When it cleared they explored the Devil's Kitchen and various other areas. The next day the *Velindra* arrived from Ilfracombe with 50 day trippers - mass tourism to the island is nothing new.

In order to avoid these visitors the two women walked to a ruined seventeenth century fort at Brazen Ward. The guns from this had been thrown into the sea by a French raiding party at some time but had been recovered 'a few years since by the tenant of the farm' who sold them to a man named Crawshaw 'who mounted them on his yacht.' One wonders where these relics of old Lundy are today?

They also visited The Battery although the 'zig zag approach is so steep that I should advise no-one to attempt that walk unless he has had some previous climbing on the island, and knows how to husband his breath.' During heavy fogs when the Lundy lighthouse couldn't be seen warning rockets were fired every 10 minutes from this site. These rockets had replaced guns 'in consequence of these being cheaper.'

The two visitors stayed on the island until the 19th of October when they were due to leave. Unfortunately they were informed that the main landing beach was not accessible and they would have to climb down the 400' high cliffs on the western side of the island to Pirates Quay. The writer describes how 'my legs trembled, and how sick with fear I felt at the inevitable before me.' Happily they got down without accident and boarded their boat arriving safely at Instow where 'we were complimented by our friends on our greatly improved looks, and healthy tanned complexions.'

So ends the account by these two intrepid Victorian women which gives us a fascinating glimpse of Lundy just over a century ago.

North Devon Journal 17.6.1999

30. The health of Barnstaple in 1898

One item of recurring news in the old *Journal*s is the '*Report of the Medical Officer of Health*'. Each district in North Devon had their own Officer and their annual surveys of the health, or lack of it, in the area make fascinating, if somewhat chilling, reading. In February 1899, for example, Dr. Mark Jackson presented his annual survey for Barnstaple over the preceding year and the *Journal* printed it verbatim.

At this date the population of the town was 13,466 and over the year there had been 293 births and 224 deaths both figures being well down on recent totals. As Jackson said, 'It is impossible not to be struck by the decline in the birth rate' as a decade earlier in 1887 there had been 404 births.

He explained this in two ways. The development of the Sticklepath estate around the newly built Shapland and Petter factory and the growth of the railway depot nearby - both of which were outside the Barnstaple borough boundaries - had attracted 'young married men from the town'. It was these men who had fast growing families - yet all the babies were being born outside of the borough. I suspect it had more to do with the increasing usage of contraception which for the first time ever was becoming more widespread and easily available, though saying this at the time was probably not politically acceptable.

Dr. Jackson then moved on to the death rate noting that 48 children under the age of one had died which equated to a mortality rate of 163 per 1000 (today it is running at about 5 per 1000). Of the 48 most died of diarrhoea - whilst 11 of them were illegitimate thus 'showing how great and considerable are the advantages or real parental supervision and responsibility' as the doctor phrased it. The high figure probably existed because of the poverty of single mothers - a reason not altogether missing today. Jackson put the total down to 'meteorological conditions' especially the combination of a hot September and wet October which might strike us as rather odd today.

One fatal case of typhoid in Silver Street was traced to defective drains whilst some 21 people had died of that scourge of the overcrowded poor - consumption. After a long and detailed account of recent scientific discoveries about the disease the Medical Officer of Health could only advise boiling all milk used in the home 'especially that used in the feeding of hand-fed children'.

His concerns over consumption were heightened by his finding that another 8 deaths were due to associated illnesses. Many cases of the disease could be traced back to the sneezes of consumptive patients which were full of bacteria. Burning used tissues and flooding sick rooms with sunshine were excellent procedures and this lent 'emphasis to the necessity of all cottages having windows, as large as circumstances will permit.' He also suggested that it would be a good thing if all private slaughterhouses could be abolished. Such places had been inspected and found clean but he still wanted their demolition as a precautionary move.

Other causes of death were seven from influenza, cancer, respiratory diseases, 'heart affections' and even 'cerebral apoplexy' - though apparently no-one had had to be removed to the Infectious Diseases Hospital Ship which had been moored for many years in the Taw estuary.

Jackson also reported that new sewers had been laid down in Silver Street and Newport the latter one designed 'to obviate the complaints which have heretofore been made in this locality of flooding of the basements of so many of the houses.' His last comment was intriguing and throws a rather worrying light on the state of healthcare in Barnstaple at the end of Victoria's long reign. 'During the past year I am glad to say the services of a trained nurse have been obtained for the town, and I have no doubt that considerable advantages will accrue to the sick poor to whom her assistance is extended.'

So ended Dr. Jackson's report - clearly the health of Barnstaple was improving slowly but one can only wonder how much better it would have been had the National Health Service, then some fifty years in the future, had been in operation.

31. A red letter day for Bideford
In Bideford's long history there have been various 'red-letter' days - the ending of the Napoleonic Wars, the granting of borough status, the outbreak of WWII - but Wednesday 7 February 1906 was perhaps just as important. On that day the town opened its new Town Hall and Library - and unveiled a statue of Charles Kingsley. Naturally the *Journal* covered these auspicious events in great detail.

Preparatory work on the Town Hall scheme had been going on for many years beginning with the council buying the site next to the end of the Long Bridge when a long established chemist's shop moved out. In 1901 the council had approached the great American philanthropist Andrew Carnegie to see if he would be interested in helping to fund a new library. In fact he offered £2200 towards the total cost of £5492 - the rest being raised by a Government loan. The work to provide the statue began in 1902 when the Mayor E.Tattersill began a subscription list to raise the £600 needed. All this behind-the-scenes work came to fruition in February 1906.

The *Journal* report noted that the new Town Hall was an extension of the old one built in 1850-51 (if one looks carefully today you will note different coloured bricks in each of the two halves). The architect was A.Dunn of Birmingham and the builder was H.Glover of Bideford. The design was described as 'Elizabethan Gothic' and the reporter was very impressed with the 'magnificent oriel window' facing the Bridge - in which the then Mayor had placed a stained glass portrait of himself!

On a slightly macabre note the *Journal* recorded how, when the foundations were being dug, some 16 human skeletons laid side by side were unearthed very near the surface. Unfortunately there was nothing with them to identify who they might be though there was a suggestion they were the remains of prisoners of war.

The new council chamber in the Town Hall was 'a noble apartment' lined with dark stained panelling and lit by a 'sixteenth century style' brass chandelier with 7 incandescent gas lights. The next door library was also lit by 6 'four light chandeliers' and furnished with reading tables and 'fifty arm chairs'. Intriguingly there was also a 'flat' in the building - presumably for the caretaker.

Whilst all this new building was going on the opportunity was taken to refurbish the old Town Hall adjoining. The main chamber had been on the ground floor next to a police holding cell and both were knocked together and then partitioned to form offices. Overall the whole scheme was adjudged a success everyone being 'struck with the stability, completeness, appropriateness and the high finish of everything in connection with the work.'

The *Journal* report then moved on to describe the events of the day which began with the unveiling of Kingsley's statue. The whole of the town was decorated with flags and an arch of evergreens had been erected at the end of the Long Bridge bearing the mottoes 'Honour to Kingsley' and 'Do lovely things, not dream them.'

The actual unveiling was carried out by Lord Clinton in the presence of the Mayor, council and the band of the local Rifle Volunteers as well as a huge crowd. After a short speech in which he praised Kingsley as both a great author and a vigorous social reformer congratulated the sculptor Joseph Whitehead for capturing Kingsley's likeness so well.

A lunch for 150 then followed in the Music Hall in Bridgeland Street where a whole succession of toasts were drunk and then the party reassembled to take part in two further ceremonies. The Library was officially opened by C.S.Carnegie using a gold key bearing the town coat-of-arms and, soon afterwards, the Mayor opened the Town Hall and both he and Lord Clinton addressed the crowds of well wishers from the balcony of the new building. The whole day ended with 'a promenade concert and a dance' in the Pannier Market in the evening - a suitably social ending to a very important day in the history of Bideford.

32. Edwardian Ilfracombe

One comes across items of local history in the oddest places. In the July 1907 edition of a long-defunct magazine *London Society* is a long article on Ilfracombe. Written by an anonymous visitor it details what was on offer for the Edwardian tourist.

It began 'Since I was here last a vast hotel has sprung up like Aladdin's palace. It is one of the most magnificent of its kind, and of an imposing magnitude for a little town like Ilfracombe.' I am unsure if this was the Cliff Hydro or the Ilfracombe Hotel. Whichever it was it was described in glowing terms; its dining room was 'vast', its drawing room 'delightful' and most importantly 'The list of prices, as compared with most hotel tariffs, is moderate.'

Having begun with praise the writer then went rapidly into censure saying 'It must be owned that in itself the town of Ilfracombe is not of the most cheering and attractive kind' with its main street apparently consisting of 'second rate inns', 'shops moderately good' and buildings 'in the equally repellent positions of construction and destruction.' Add to this the smallness of the public baths and 'public reading rooms not over well supplied with periodicals' and one clearly gets the impression of seediness. The only saving grace was the churches and chapels 'in great abundance' this allowing the writer to say 'the Ilfracombe mind has manifestly a great proclivity towards ecclesiastical distinctions.'

He in fact ends his list of shortcomings with the memorable sentence 'Ilfracombe is not a gem set in a rude casket, but it is something rude and unformed set in the loveliest and most glorious of caskets.' This 'casket' was the surrounding countryside with its breathtaking views. To the North was South Wales and out to sea was Lundy apparently then much visited by 'Sunday sportsmen' shooting snipe and woodcock.

A ride by 'hotel omnibus' or the 'mail coach' to Barnstaple was not to be missed especially as the latter would 'sweep you through a wild lovely valley, which suits very with the story of an awful murder which was committed here many years ago.' One oddity that has probably now declined was the importance placed on natural history. As the writer notes - 'Socially it is everything here. You are hardly fit to live unless you know everything about anemones.' Every house was said to have its aquarium and there was laver on every table if the writer is to be believed.

After a day's beachcombing for specimens to fill their aquariums Edwardians apparently liked nothing better than a stroll around Capstone Hill 'which is the joy and delight of the people of Ilfracombe.' Also highly recommended were the local beaches with the writer commenting on the beauty and utility of the 'Tunnel' leading to two coves, the one on the right for ladies, the left for gentlemen. (When did they become desegregated?)

The article finishes with a very contemporary sounding discussion as to how the hoteliers and shopkeepers of the town were trying to extend the 'season' all through the year. The writer reckoned that they shouldn't hide the fact that strong winds were common - rather they should be made much of and referred to as 'bracing' in advertisements - I don't know how well they succeeded in this!

So ended this early version of our 'travel correspondent' with a promise to write about Exmoor Clearly he found both good and bad points about Ilfracombe - one wonders what he would write today if he could somehow return 90 years on?
North Devon Journal 15.7.1999

33. The silver screen on canvas

The history of the cinema in North Devon has yet to be written. Anyone who does try to discover material about the early years of moving pictures in this area will soon discover that the first shows were given in portable canvas-walled cinemas as part of the entertainment provided by travelling fairs.

Obviously large specialised buildings such as cinemas were not built overnight especially when the level of demand in these early days of film was uncertain. Proprietors of fairs, however, had large tents as part of their normal equipment and these could easily double as cinemas. Unfortunately there had been a spate of fatal accidents with early film projectors which had a tendency to burst into flame after any extended use owing to the absence of any cooling apparatus and the Government had passed an Act of Parliament in 1909 called The Cinematograph Act. This legislation set out that anyone wishing to give a film show had to notify the police in writing at least two days before under penalty of a maximum fine of £20 if they failed to do so. These two days could then be used by the police to inspect the equipment and, depending on whether they thought it safe or not, give their approval for the show to go ahead.

In October 1910 William Hancock described as 'the well known show proprietor' arrived in Barnstaple to attend the annual Fair. With him came his brother-in-law John Jones who ran a 'cinematograph exhibition' as one of the attractions. Jones had a licence from Devon County Council to give film shows but even so he still required the approval of the local police at wherever he stopped.

In Barnstaple he set up his show tent along with the rest of the Fair on a site near the present Civic Centre - where its presence was noticed by Chief Constable Eddy of the Barnstaple borough police force. When Eddy asked James why he had not applied for a licence James rather lamely claimed it was an oversight on his part. Eddy then said he would have to 'take proceedings against him' and even though Jones asked him not to the case quickly came up in the local magistrates' court.

At the court hearing the Chief Constable said he had been told that William Hancock had been to see him in connection with getting a licence the day before the Fair began. He had gone and inspected the equipment and found it satisfactory but the law demanded that two day's notice be given. In mitigation Hancock claimed he had gone to the police station two days before the Fair's opening but Eddy had not been there and unfortunately Hancock didn't leave a written request for permission as he should have done.

The case, therefore, only really hinged on the technical point that one day's notice had been given instead of two - and on this basis Hancock asked that only a light penalty be imposed, adding that his having to attend court on his brother-in-law's behalf had already cost him £3 in lost income. The bench, however, were very aware of the danger of holding film shows 'in a crowded place like Barnstaple Fair' but as they knew Mr.Hancock as an upright citizen they only imposed a fine of £1 plus costs.

North Devon Journal 19.11.1998

34. The School Medical Officer
Through the kindness of a friend I have recently been able to read a fascinating little booklet entitled 'Report of the School Medical Officer for the Borough of Barnstaple for 1924' written by Dr.S.R.Gibbs. Such officers were charged with inspecting all

the schoolchildren in their area in order to catch the first signs of any illnesses early and tackle them before they became worse. Each year they prepared their report which went to the local Education Authority and though one might expect them to make dry reading they are actually extremely enlightening about living conditions then existing.

This particular report begins with a general overview of numbers of school-children within Barnstaple and observes that many 'very young' children had been allowed to enter the town's infant schools. This was due to their being plenty of spaces available due to the 'lean years' during and just after the First World War when, not unnaturally, birth rates fell dramatically.

The medical officer thought this early entry had helped the children - especially over the preceding two years which had been very wet. They had 'been better off at School than in the streets, and the very limited accommodation of their own houses' - which clearly indicates the problem of overcrowding at this date.

Dr.Gibbs then offers a statistical breakdown of the year. Some 124 children were 'found unclean' with 5 being 'verminous' out of 2709 examined. The doctor wrote 'I again would impress on the Authority the necessity of providing at the earliest date public Baths, Washhouses' as in the poor areas there was often just 'one tap in the backyard having to serve for 2 houses.' Indeed he was full of admiration for mothers who managed to keep their children clean under these conditions - although the 'fortunate fashion of bobbing the hair' had meant that lice infestation in girls was less common!

More serious were the cases of tuberculosis. Some 12 cases had been identified and they had been sent to an 'open air school' at Torrington for 'Fresh air and good feeding' though the doctor experienced the 'greatest difficulty' in persuading parents to let their children go.

Some 5 children were found to have ringworm on their head with another 5 having it on their bodies whilst 4 had scabies. The scalp sufferers had apparently been sent to Exeter to receive X-ray treatment for the condition - which sounds extremely dangerous although Gibbs reckoned that 'in all the cases treated there had been no ill effects.' A case of rickets referred to the medical officer by the NSPCC had been sent to the Bristol Orthopaedic Centre and the child had returned 'enormously improved'. It was noted that the sufferer had not missed any schooling as this was provided in the hospital.

The School Dentist, Mabel Inder, reported how she had removed 1152 teeth during the year. The use of general anaesthetic in 45 cases was especially helpful 'as no other method of extraction' from 'really septic mouths' was so useful - which is a chilling reminder of just how bad tooth care used to be only 70 years ago.

The last entries concern those children with mental handicaps. The use of language was blunt in that 'There have been 2 Imbeciles notified to the Authority, both girls.' Apparently there was a special school for these children in Grosvenor Street, Barnstaple. Hearteningly the doctor added that one boy from this school 'has recently gained a high place in Art Examinations in the Country since leaving School.'

To the historian all this is fairly small beer but because it deals with the lives of ordinary people it has a fascination not to be found elsewhere - as I hope comes over in this article.
North Devon Journal 20.1.2000

35. Of limestone and limekilns

I have written before about the lime burning industry of North Devon and the many kilns it has left behind. The importation of limestone from South Wales and its manufacture into a valuable dressing for poor soils was a major employer in the eighteenth and nineteenth centuries. Records of the trade, however, are scarce and I was intrigued to recently come across an article written in 1934 that evidently drew on the memories of those still alive who had been involved in the industry.

Apparently most of the limestone itself came from Caldey Island, three miles from Tenby and Worms Head in South Wales although local deposits were also exploited. Once quarried and broken up into manageable lumps it was shipped in cargoes of between 60 and 90 tons to North Devon by 'as hardy a race of sailormen this silver-coasted isle of ours has ever produced.'

The ships were known as 'muffies', a corruption of hermaphrodite they being a combination of ketch and schooner. They made up to three round trips a week the crew being paid the princely sum of 50 to 60p a voyage. On arrival in North Devon they were unloaded direct onto beaches or river beds by men and women - the Appledore women being especially famous for their strength (and violence to those who offended them!) These 'heavers' received 10 to 12p a day for their hard labour which was poor reward for a job that could often lead to serious injury - as many reports in the contemporary *Journal* bear witness.

The ships were mainly built in the shipbuilding yards that lined the Torridge and the article names some - the *Lady Rolle, Swan, Two Sisters* and *Kitty Ann*. A rather odder one was the *Newton* which was a French boat captured during the Napoleonic Wars and pushed into service in the lime trade.

These ships also brought in the coal needed to fuel the kilns, local culm not really being good enough for the job. Indeed this absence of coal was the main reason why North Devon never developed as a major industrial area.

Once the limestone had been 'roasted' in the kilns, which could take some time, it was collected by local farmers and their pack horses. They aimed to arrive at the kiln from 5 a.m. on - where they would cook their breakfast strips of bacon on the still hot limestone. This simple repast was helped down with 'liberal pulls from their cider kegs.' Taken home to their fields the limestone was left in piles until well 'crumbled' - and then spread on the heavy clay soils of the area to 'sweeten' them.

Although limekilns were common all around the North Devon coast the article reckoned 'the great centre of lime burning' was at Vellator in Braunton. Here there were five large kilns adjoining the River Caen which, even by 1934, had all disappeared.

The most important inland site was at Venn in Landkey which relied on the local limestone quarried at Codden Hill which employed up to twenty men at any one time. The article notes that the quarry had flooded and 'is now one of the beauty spots of the district, especially in May, when the adjoining cherry orchards are in bloom.'

The industry came to an end when artificial fertilisers began to be introduced. Not only were they cheaper but they were more efficient and gave better results. The coming of the railways to the area meant that they were cheaper to transport as well. When the last limestone ships sailed is hard to tell but today, as in 1934, the only reminders of this vital trade are the derelict and decaying limekilns around our coast - the mute reminders of a once vital industry.

North Devon Journal 23.12.1999

TRANSPORT

36. Heroic Appledore men

The North Devon coast was long feared by sailors as a nautical graveyard. After the establishment of a lifeboat at Appledore, however, crews were at least given a fighting chance for survival as is shown by events in 1836.

In the early hours of November 29th a 'hurricane' swept in from the Atlantic and across North Devon pushing a number of vessels into danger. At 9 a.m. two schooners were seen trapped on Bideford Bar at the entrance to the estuaries of the Taw and Torridge. One was the *Excellent* of Fowey and the other the *Henrietta* of Plymouth. A small gig boat set out from Appledore and arriving alongside the *Excellent* got her exhausted crew into their own boats and towed them back to Appledore 'where they found a warm-hearted people to administer to their wants.'

It was thought that the crew of the *Henrietta* had already abandoned ship but 'it was discovered by a good glass that six men were suspended in the fore and main rigging.' The large lifeboat was dragged across the Northam Burrows from its shed but 'it was deemed too perilous an undertaking to launch her.' In fact the usual crew weren't willing to set out owing to an accident that had occurred a little time before during which they had lost all confidence in the seaworthiness of the lifeboat.

By 2 p.m., however, things were becoming desperate and Thomas Burnard, the secretary of the 'Shipwrecked Institution', offered a reward of £20 to any crew who volunteered to go to the aid of the *Henrietta's* crew.

At this five men stepped forward - Captain Thomas Day, John Mayne, William Eastman, David Hooper and William Smallridge. The lifeboat was then 'instantly launched' and the men began their long row out to the stricken ship. About the same time another two boats also set out from Instow under the command of Joshua Williams and Edward J.England.

After a heroic struggle the Appledore men reached the *Henrietta*, took off the six half-drowned crew and with the help of the Instow boats finally reached shore 'in a complete state of exhaustion' - to the cheers of the entire population of the village.

Two days later the officers of the 'Shipwrecked Institution' met at Berwick's Hotel in Appledore and awarded votes of thanks and money to the rescue teams. Each man in the lifeboat got £5 each though three declined to take the money. The Instow crews were given £1 each though again the two captains wouldn't take the cash.

The rescued sailors were given new clothes and a warm bed by the Appledore villagers and within a few days were sent home via the Plymouth coach with a present of cash each - the total coming to £16. The *Henrietta* was a total loss but the *Excellent* was got into harbour with little damage.

The following week the *Journal* published a letter from the *Henrietta's* captain Pascoe Buchan wherein he thanked the sailors who had 'at the risk of your lives' come to the rescue of him and his crew. In addition the editor printed a poem written by 'A Lover of True Courage' which contained the stirring lines,

'The bark's deserted amidst the howling blast,
The seamen clinging to her tottering mast;
Piercing the shriek which in despair of life
In echo's wafted by the tempest's strife;
Their moments numbered - hope seem'd idle there,
Nor aught assuaged the mind save black despair.
Amidst this anxious awful, solemn scene,
Behold! the life boat suddenly is seen,
With hardy seamen bound to save,
Or perish in the briny wave.

Dramatic times - though of course these events have been repeated many times since - and not always with such a successful outcome.
North Devon Journal 22.4.1999

37. The wreck of the Lochlibo

North Devon's coast has been littered with the wreckage from thousands of ships over the centuries. Most occurred at the height of storms but one in 1859 came in calm weather before an audience of hundreds.

On 10th February 1859 Captain Owen Thomas had left Newport in South Wales in his barque the *Lochlibo*. The ship which was valued at £8000 had a burthen of 1060 tons, a crew of 24 and was the property of John Martin and Sons of Dublin. It had been chartered by a firm in Rio de Janeiro to carry 1300 tons of coal to South America - a voyage that was to be its last.

Leaving Newport Captain Thomas had taken a pilot on board but the weather was against them. Indeed the ship didn't really make any headway until the 23rd, and then took 3 days to reach Lundy where the pilot was discharged.

A little later Thomas was off Padstow when a gale blew up and he was carried backwards striking some sunken rocks off Hartland at 6 a.m. The sea lifted the vessel and smashed it back on to the rocks three times which was enough to cause major leaks; indeed within minutes there was 4' of water in the hold. The captain ordered all hands to the pumps and had a flag hoisted to show he wanted a pilot to come aboard and help.   A passing vessel, the *Edwin Cary*, sent a pilot aboard - at which point there was 14 feet of water in the hold, an inoperative helm and the ship was drifting helplessly up the North Devon coastline. Faced with this rapidly worsening situation the pilot tried to run the ship ashore at Ilfracombe but by now the vessel was unmanageable and he thus ordered the crew to take to the boats. This they did leaving only the captain on board.

The stricken vessel accompanied by the crew in the lifeboats began drifting ashore. By now the weather was calm and huge crowds gathered to watch her, many of them 'speculating upon the place of her contact with the rocks, and the period of her fate.' In addition they also discussed 'the fate or folly or whatever other cause (many of their speculations being anything but charitable) which had brought so fine a ship into such a hopeless predicament' - suspicions heightened by the fact that the captain refused any help from the local men who rowed out to stricken ship. The currents actually carried her to Lee - to where she was followed by large numbers of people.

When just 200 yards offshore the ship's carpenter, John Pickard of Bideford, was ordered back on board 'to scuttle the ship by cutting holes in her deck, hoping thereby to keep her upright when she struck with the view of saving as much as possible.' In fact the ship sank into 'a sort of rock cradle' where at high tide the waves broke over her. This allowed salvage teams to remove large amounts of her 'gear and stores' including the beef and pork loaded for the crew's provisions. Whilst this was going on Lieutenant Jones and his coastguard men were said to be 'constantly on duty about the wreck' to deter looters.

A few weeks later an official investigation under Captain Harris from London was held into the case - the first in North Devon under the Merchant Seaman's Act of 1854. Captain Thomas recounted his actions noting especially that the offers of help came too late - and that many of them came from men who were 'intoxicated and very disorderly'. The hearing lasted 2 days and ended with the chairman saying 'the captain stood clear of any charge of wilful negligence or incompetency.'

These events have long been forgotten and the story gone into the limbo of history but wrecks still occur around our coasts though, happily, they are a very rare event though one can imagine huge crowds still turning out today if such a tragedy occurred so close inshore again

38. A drunken Captain

North Devon has a long tradition of producing famous sailors - from Sir Richard Grenville to Sir Francis Chichester the area can be proud of its seagoing men. Sadly not all local mariners were quite so impressive. In May 1867 *Journal* readers were greeted with the headline 'Serious charge against a ship's captain'.

The 'captain' was Robert Dummett, master of the 425 ton ship *Mangosteen*, who came from Braunton, whilst the 'charge' was brought by the Bristol Local Marine Board where the hearing was held. Robert did not appear to answer the charge but his employers William Nicholson & Sons of Sunderland who owned the *Mangosteen* went ahead to present their case. Simply expressed they alleged that Robert had been drunk whilst in charge of his ship.

As Robert was not present the Board members allowed a letter from him to be read out. Dated 'April 30 Swansea' in it he admitted to receiving the summons to appear but he reckoned it was 'utterly impossible for me to attend' as he had no money for the journey. He added further 'My wife and family are in a state of starvation not having received any money from my employers since last September.' Robert had eight children as well as the wife so one can perhaps sympathise with his inability to travel. He went on to say that his Master's 'certificate' was in the Cape of Good Hope where 'being in a hurry to go on board the steamer it must have been missed.'

The prosecuting solicitor reckoned the letter to be 'a mere excuse for the defendant's non-attendance.' He went on to detail the charges. Robert had left Swansea on 26 January 1866 carrying coal to Chile. Arriving at Valparaiso on 12 May Robert immediately 'went ashore, gave himself to drink, and did not write to the owners to inform them of his arrival at that port.' Indeed he had only contacted them once during the whole voyage and that letter 'was scarcely legible.'

Additionally during his five day alcoholic binge at Valparaiso the ship's steward became ill and the Captain cruelly 'put him on the beach and left him there.' Calling in at a port called Caldera he again became drunk. He then continued down the coast of South America only to arrive at the Falkland Islands where the *Mangosteen* foundered and sank. Eventually being repatriated he refused to tell the ship's owners any details of what had happened and point-blank refused to give any information about 'the moneys he had received' for his cargo of coal.

Evidence about Robert's drunkenness came from two crew members Daniel Braden and John Morgan who recalled how their captain had 'whilst suffering from delirium tremens jumped overboard, but was picked up by the crew, who were obliged to put him in irons and confine him to his cabin.' It must have been an interesting voyage if nothing else!

Faced with such damaging evidence the Board rapidly found Robert 'guilty of gross acts of drunkeness' which had left him 'totally incompetent' to control the ship under his command - and accordingly they immediately cancelled his Captain's certificate. Clearly Robert wasn't one of North Devon's most illustrious sailors!

North Devon Journal 4.11.2005

39. Grand plan for steam ferry, tram and canal

Appledore and Instow today are relatively quiet places catering for holidaymakers, the retired and second home owners for the most part. In the last century, however, there was a grand plan to link the two via a steam ferry, which in turn would form one end of a tramway to Westward Ho! - where it could also be used to bolster the pebble ridge.

It began with a public meeting held in the National School Room at Appledore on Saturday April 1 1876, 'pursuant to notice Circulated about the Parish, to consider the expediency of having a Steam Ferry.' The chairman was Admiral Dowell and he called on various local gentlemen to give their views on the proposal. Amongst them was Captain Molesworth, a man who was very closely involved with many of the schemes to develop Westward Ho!

The overall feeling was in favour of the scheme and a 12 man committee was set up to consider the practicalities - with an agreement to have their first meeting just four days later. Clearly Victorians didn't hang about. At the same time it was agreed to hold another public meeting to discuss 'the proposals of protecting the Burrows and forming a Tramway from Appledore to Westward Ho! across the Burrows.'

At the committee meeting four days later the members, along with two Torridge river pilots, 'inspected the stream at lowest tide and the various points proposed as loading places for establishing an improved Ferry from Instow to Appledore.' Two possible landing sites were identified in Instow - the old stone pier and the railway station. If the former were to be chosen 'a short Iron Pier, Hard or landing stages' would be needed but this would be cheaper than the latter which would need 'a canal and a landing, hard or pier' some 400 yards in length. This rather sounds like the pontoon extending out from today's Yacht Club.

In Appledore three sites were examined including the slip at the bottom of Bude Street, the point opposite Meeting Street and one on the rocks near the Custom House. The first would cost nothing, the second needed a new jetty and the third would be part of the tramway scheme.

After careful consideration the committee plumped for a link between Instow station and the Custom House believing that the scheme 'will benefit the whole Parish and give employment to the people.' They also stressed its feasibility and 'the necessity of carrying out the project with as little delay as possible.'

Three days later the meeting was held to discuss the protection of the Burrows and the Appledore to Westward Ho! tramway. After a few speeches the gentlemen present came to a momentous decision - to hold another meeting on April 22! They also set up a second committee to examine the tramway and suggested protection for the Burrows.

This rather weak compromise heralded the end of the great hopes expressed at the various meetings. Indeed the discussion on April 22 ended even more prosaically when it was noted that the committee was unanimous 'that something must be done for the protection of the Burrows.' This vague 'something' appeared to consist solely of a tramway from Gray Sand to Westward Ho! via Sandymere. A canal running alongside this link was also put forward - presumably to give easy access to the Taw and Torridge by-passing the notorious sand bar at the mouth of the estuary.

In order to encourage an entrepreneur to take on the scheme the committee agreed to offer the land required to them for free but in the event virtually nothing happened. The Instow-Appledore ferry continued to be a rowing boat, the Appledore-Westward Ho! tram link took another 25 years to arrive - and the canal never materialised. So ended this brief flare of local enthusiasm - a pity as a steam ferry would have been a real tourist attraction today.

North Devon Journal 20.7.2000

40. Drink and boats do not mix

The River Torridge is an extremely attractive river and can often be seen crowded with yachts, water skiers, fishermen and nature lovers. It does, however, have a dark side which is revealed only occasionally. In June 1885 this came into clear view when it claimed the lives of five young men from Appledore.

Two of the men had sailed up to Bideford about 8 p.m. one Saturday evening and there met six friends. Visiting various public houses they were, three hours later, 'more or less under the influence of the liquor they had imbibed', indeed two were 'awfully drunk'. In this state they had all climbed into the boat for the journey home.

They had very nearly reached the village without incident when the helmsman attempted to tack direct into the Quay but was caught, with his sails full, by the wind 'which was blowing half a gale.' All eight passengers were thrown into the sea - and five of them drowned.

At the inquest held the next day in the Royal George public house in the village they were named as John Scobling (22), John Berry (20), John Giddy (21), W.Gregory (23) and W.Balcom (20). William and Thomas Berry and Edwin Richards were the survivors. All were unmarried and the three bodies that had then been recovered were identified by P.c.Parker the local policeman who knew them all well.

At the inquest Edwin Richards, who was a sailor and had been in control of the boat, recounted how he and Balcom had hired a boat from John Fishwick (the Instow ferryman) and sailed to Bideford to buy some goods. Here they had met with their friends and the party went to 'different public houses' although he only drank two pints of beer himself. Scobling, however, who had already managed to smash a window that evening fell on the Quay 'and hit his head.' His companions picked him up and carried him to the boat where they all got in and set sail at 11.35 p.m.

There was no 'skylarking' on the way back and they made good time until the disastrous move which pitched them into the river. Richards and William Berry managed to swim to a nearby boat and began shouting for help. They could only see one of their group, John Giddy, who was calling out 'Lord have mercy upon me.' Their calls were answered when Isaac Short and his son came to their rescue and ferried them to Instow.

Poor Richards was closely questioned by several of the jurors who were obviously extremely experienced boatmen and they all remarked that 'the course adopted by the witness was very dangerous and injudicious'. Mr.Fishwick, however, who had rented the boat to Richards, defended him saying that all the party knew about boats and 'all were equally to blame'.

Isaac Short deposed how he had been in bed when his wife heard screams for help and woke him. Pausing only to put on his 'drawers and stockings' he and his son ran to the beach and put off in a boat though it was 'blowing hard' at the time. He then described how he rescued the men.

The coroner in his summing up said how sad it was that five young men 'had been hurried into Eternity in the way they had' although clearly their drinking had been a major component in their fate. He went on to say, rather needlessly, 'He hoped it would be a life-long lesson to those who were saved.' The jury quickly returned the obvious verdict - 'Accidentally Drowned'. They added a recommendation that the conduct of Short and his son should be brought to the attention of the Royal Humane Society though whether anything came of this I am unsure. Sadly only three bodies were recovered from the river, the other two had probably 'been washed over the bar' and thus 'no hope is entertained of recovering them.' A sad end to a cheerful evening.

North Devon Journal 30.12.1999

41. The unforgiving sea

The old hymn 'For those in peril on the sea' has a special resonance here in North Devon where so many ships and sailors have come to grief around our jagged coastline. In April 1899 a huge gale swept up the Bristol Channel and over the two days it lasted it spread death and destruction all along the beaches and cliffs of this area. The *Journal*'s report is peppered with headlines such as 'Wreck at Saunton; Two lives lost', 'Supposed

Foundering off Lundy Island' and 'Striking Scene at Appledore - Many casualties'.

At Saunton, for example, the *Joseph and Thomas*, a ketch from Bude manned by Captain Shazell and two crew members got into trouble. The boat had left Port Talbot loaded with coal for Penrhyn but huge waves drove it off course and Shazell determined to make for Ilfracombe. Sadly the vessel couldn't make harbour and was blown down the coast towards Saunton.

By now all the sails had been swept away and waves were breaking right over the deck. Shazell climbed into the rigging and one of the crew, Fred Davis 'an expert swimmer', leapt overboard to try for shore but never reached it. As the ship began to sink Shazell shouted to the other crew member John Couch 'Good bye John! It is all up with us. God save me!' - and was never seen alive again. Couch grabbed a lifebuoy and was found some time later bobbing about in the sea near the Braunton lighthouse. He 'seemed to be dead' but after a local man John Isaac waded in and dragged him ashore he was found to be still alive and, taken to Saunton Hotel, he slowly recovered.

At Ilfracombe a Brixham trawler the *Olive and Mary* with a four man crew got into difficulties but they were rescued by the town's lifeboat after heavy seas smashed everything on deck, carried away both their sails and fishing gear and left them exhausted.

At Appledore the 'river and bay was one mass of breakers', and during the storm many vessels broke their moorings and drifted ashore on Instow beach. Captain Dart in the *Gannet* (the Lundy supply boat) saved four of the crew of the *Spitfire* of Ramsgate. This was after a German steamer came up to their doomed craft and threw ropes to them 'which the crew fastened around their bodies and then jumped into the water, and were thus dragged through the sea' until Dart came up and took them aboard.

Another Brixham trawler the *Vivid* under Captain Plumridge managed to limp into Ilfracombe and reported seeing a Norwegian vessel in a sinking state off Lundy. Three men were on her 'without hats and coats', only two had lifebelts on whilst the third 'appeared to be praying'. All were 'screaming for help and looked quite worn out'. Plumridge tried to approach but couldn't and the last they saw of the men was when their vessel 'disappeared from view all at once in the trough of a sea'. Plumridge went on to report how some fourteen steamers were anchored off Lundy seeking what shelter they could.

Over the next few weeks news drifted in of other losses to North Devon ships and sailors. Thus, for example, Captain Jones of Clovelly returned home after losing his vessel *The Rival* just off Cork in Southern Ireland. All in all it was a gale to remember - and one that showed both the power of the sea along with the bravery and fortitude of local seamen and lifeboatmen.

42. The railway that never was

It is well known that the last railway built in North Devon was the Bideford, Westward Ho! and Appledore line which began life in 1901. What is less well known is that a later one was planned but never constructed. This was the Bideford and Hartland Light Railway - and in March 1905 a Public Inquiry was held in Bideford Town Hall as to whether the company behind the plan should be granted a licence to build it.

At this packed hearing the first to speak was a barrister, J.A. Hawke, who was employed to put the case for the line. He began by pointing out that the railway would run through 'one of the largest tracts now remaining unrailwayed in this country.' The line, if licensed, would join up with the existing London and South Western Railway line at Landcross and thus be linked to the national rail system. Support for the line was 'practically unanimous' and all the parishes through which the line would run had sent in petitions in favour of it - many of them pointing out the expected improvements it would bring in some detail.

Thus Hartland supported it as it would lower the price of fertilisers for local farmers. Having it carted from Bideford station meant the transport cost was 10/- (50p) per ton which they expected to fall to 3/- (15p) if the rail line were built. Similar reductions would follow for coal.

Clovelly and Bucks Mills wrote in claiming that apart from tourism they 'were practically supported by fishing' and they foresaw benefits from a faster and cheaper form of transport for their fish. Apparently at this date if there was a large catch transport by road was so inefficient that part of the catch had to be left 'to rot upon the beach'. Indeed the industry was in virtual collapse - but the arrival of the railway was expected to reinvigorate it. Another benefit was that more tourists would arrive as getting to the two villages was very expensive and only 'those whose pockets were large enough' could currently make the journey. In addition local timber would be able to be moved cheaply. 'Agents for the landed proprietors' all supported the railway as it would allow them to sell their products at far more competitive prices.

Another reason advanced in support of the scheme was the proposed construction of a new 'building estate at Bucks Mills' which being 'beautifully situated' was where 'retired people would, it was thought, desire to live' and where tourists would stay in a new large hotel.

The barrister was followed by Joseph Davis an expert on rail traffic flows who had worked on the expected costs and income of the line. He reckoned that there would be some 55,000 passengers a year who would generate some £17,980 in ticket sales. On top of this he added £300 from 'sale of refreshments' and £350 from 'contracts for mails'. In addition there would be income from freight which he reckoned at about £6300 a year. William Foxlee of Westminster then gave the costs which he based on the construction of some 15 miles of line along with stations at Hartland, Clovelly Dykes, Bucks Cross, Hoops Inn, Landcross plus improvements at Bideford. According to his calculations the total cost would be £143,391.

After listening to all this supportive evidence the Inquiry chairman announced that subject to one amendment they would grant a licence for the railway. This was greeted with 'Loud applause' from the listeners but as we all know the line was never built. We can only speculate what would have happened if it had been constructed. Would it have disappeared in the Beeching closures in the 1960s or would it have struggled on to become a major tourist draw today - or even a beautiful extension to the Tarka line? - alas we will never know.

North Devon Journal 4.6.2004

MILITARY

43. Bishop Tawton's yeoman army of the past

Four hundred years ago our Elizabethan ancestors had no permanent or standing army. Instead they relied on a national militia to which, theoretically, every Englishman between the ages of 16 and 60 belonged. Training was carried out at least once every year when the men were 'mustered'.

To check that everyone turned up the local parish constables would compile lists of the able-bodied in their parish and what weapons they possessed. These lists were sent to the 'muster-master' and, luckily for the local historian, many still survive. A Devon list for 1569 has survived and been published. Only 25 parishes were omitted and the total number of militia men came to 17,778 - a force strong in numbers but almost certainly weak in training.

For each parish the richest inhabitants were listed first along with the arms they were to supply - the idea being that their arms would go to the poorer men who couldn't afford the basic kit which consisted of a pikeman's light armour called a corslet consisting of metal back and breast plates held together with straps along with a 'murrion' or morion which was a visorless iron helmet.

From the 1569 listing we can take Bishops Tawton as an example. The village as a whole had to supply one corslet, one pike, one caliver or gun and one morion. These 'parish arms' would most likely have been kept in the church - the only public building most communities had at that date. Other arms would have come from the central government arsenals when and where needed.

Eight rich men were listed who would have had to supply other weapons including the expensive arquebuses - an early type of gun. They were followed by lists of the 'habell menne' in the parish. Thus thirty four archers are listed with nineteen 'harquebusiers', nine pikemen and seven billmen - these latter would have carried axes or large edged weapons.

It is interesting to note even at this early date the numbers of gunners as against the numbers of archers. A good archer took years to train whereas anyone could point a gun in the right direction and fire. Even by the mid-sixteenth century the glorious age of the English longbow which saw such victories as Agincourt and Crecy was rapidly disappearing.

Bishops Tawton was a fairly typical parish both in terms of numbers and weapons. Other parishes were poorer; for example, tiny Landcross was listed as having just one archer and two arquebusiers - whilst some were richer. One of these was Alwington with its seventeen footmen and two light horse or cavalrymen armed with pistols and lance - a rarity only found in the wealthiest parishes or where there was a rich man residing.

This system of local militias continued sporadically until the nineteenth century though it had by then become more efficient. It is perhaps not unkind to suggest that England was lucky that the Spanish Armada never actually landed troops on our shores. How would our part-time militiamen have stood up to a powerful force of well-armed and trained regular troops?

North Devon Journal 26.1.1989

44. The North Devon Yeomanry Cavalry

In the last decade of the eighteenth century and first of the nineteenth Britain was locked in mortal combat with Republican France then ruled by the charismatic Napoleon. The threat of imminent invasion was taken very seriously by both the Army and the government and many steps were taken to forestall a successful landing. Circular forts known as Martello Towers were erected, lookouts posted and naval patrols in the Channel stepped up.

The populace of Britain was called upon to arm and train themselves much in the way that a later generation joined the Home Guard. The lead in North Devon was taken by Lord Rolle who in 1793 began recruiting volunteers for the newly formed North Devon Yeomanry Cavalry. Response was good and the regiment quickly took shape and started training in earnest.

Records of these early days are not voluminous - the situation was critical and actions counted more than words and bureaucracy. Nevertheless the North Devon Record Office now possesses several muster rolls for the regiment from around this time. One, dated December 1813, is written in a fine hand on two very large sheets of paper. It begins by listing six staff officers including the regiment's Colonel - Lord Rolle who came from Stevenstone - along with his aide Lt.Colonel J.Fortescue from Buckland Filleigh. The four other staff officers all came from Torrington and included the two regimental surgeons, Thomas Colley and Edmund Caddy.

Nine troops made up the regiment, each of which was based around a local base town. The nine were Bideford, Torrington, Fremington, Swimbridge, Stevenstone, Hatherleigh, Sheepwash, Monkleigh and Holsworthy. The average strength of each troop was 66, although Holsworthy for some unexplained reason only mustered 47.

The 66 men of the Bideford troop consisted of 63 troopers and three officers. For each man his home settlement was given and these show just how wide the catchment area was for this troop. Twenty-four men came from Bideford itself, two from Hartland, eight from Parkham, four from Clovelly, two from Abbotsham, one from Appledore and even one from Morwenstow as well as many other places in the area.

The names of these men are still well known in the vicinity. The three Majors for example were Messrs.Chanter, Willcock and Tardrew - all from Bideford. Among the troopers were William Paddon, Michael Crang, William May, John Prouse, William Williams, John Woollacott and John Hedden.

From other records we know that the uniform of these part-time soldiers was fairly splendid - a scarlet jacket faced with silver lace, white breeches and black riding boots. Whether there was any head-gear or not is uncertain but they probably wore helmets of some sort. These colourfully uniformed men rode their own horses and were armed with a sword and a pistol whilst each troop also had twelve carbines to draw on.

These part-time soldiers were never called on to act against an enemy invader - indeed their war was a very quiet one consist-

ing as it did of mainly reviews and training exercises. Their first taste of action came, somewhat ironically, when they were called on to suppress a riot by starving townspeople in Bideford in 1816 - a story I have dealt with elsewhere. One wonders how they would have coped against the professional armies of France if Napoleon had ever managed to cross the Channel?
Bideford Gazette 11.12.1981

45. Hatherleigh celebrates the end of the Crimean War
The Crimean War saw the strange alliance of Britain, France and Turkey take on Russia in an odd-shaped peninsula of land in the Black Sea. The reasons for the war are not easily explained and most people today only remember it for two things; the pioneering work of Florence Nightingale and the ill-fated 'Charge of the Light Brigade'. The war in fact lasted from 1853 until 1856 and although largely forgotten today saw a contemporary surge of patriotism sweep across the country. When the war finally ended celebrations were held throughout Britain.

Typical were those held in Hatherleigh on June 5, 1856. The 'National Day of Rejoicing' had been a week earlier but Hatherleigh had put its back 'for several reasons of convenience.' The *Journal*, which covered the day in some detail, applauded the townspeople for being 'determined by a unanimous effort to make the proceedings worthy the cause.'

A 24-man committee was set up to plan the day's events which included three members of the Bulleid family, two Snells and two Hoopers amongst their number. They organised a packed day which began 'at an early hour' with a squadron of the North Devon Mounted Rifles riding into town behind their band which was playing 'Cheer boys! Cheer.' If this wasn't enough to wake the sleeping inhabitants we read that the cavalrymen 'at given distances rent the air by discharging volleys from their firearms.' To complete the cacophony the church bells began tolling.

The entire town was decorated with arches of evergreen branches whilst every house 'however humble had its own fanciful design.' The townspeople seem to have been very keen on banners bearing mottoes. One read 'Peace brings Hope and

Plenty'. Union Jacks and French tricolors were everywhere with one house boasting the initials VA and NE worked in flowers. These stood for Victoria and Albert and Napoleon and Eugenie - the heads of state of Britain and France. Over the schoolmaster's house fluttered the flag of St.George whilst the local builder S.Hooper had prepared a double arch with two banners reading, at some length, 'The British Lion, may he never rise in anger, nor lie down in fear' and 'Three cheers for the red, white and blue.'

The Post Office carried a two sided banner which read on one side 'Loyalty to our Queen, Submission to our Laws, Happiness to our People' and on the other 'Hurrah for the Roast Beef of Old England.' The postmaster, Mr.Hooper, had also erected a plaster statue of Queen Victoria 'crowned with a wreath of olive, and in her hands full ears of corn.'

The high point of the day was the procession through the town led by the North Devon Mounted Rifles. They were followed by 'Mr John Strang with his cock'd hat, sash etc in the dress of a General' though I think it safe to say he was not a real officer. The town constables then appeared either side of the Portreeve of Hatherleigh on a horse. The band of the Mounted Rifles came next - just in front of the Organising Committee and local clergy, magistrates and doctors. A variety of agricultural workers carrying their tools and tradesmen 'with emblems of their profession' came along next. They were followed by four young men 'carrying a chair tastefully trimmed, with a child sitting in it' who presumably was the equivalent of the 'Princess' we see at Carnivals today. She was accompanied by the Hatherleigh Band who marched in front of 'The labouring classes and families, near 800 in number.' This huge crowd were followed by the Exbourne Band whilst the tail of the long procession saw the men of the local Odd Fellows Lodge walking behind their 'admired Banner.'

After touring the whole town more than 1000 people sat down to a banquet around the market place. Here, in staggered sittings, they feasted on a meal of beef, pudding, bread and beer. A little later 250 of the 'most respectable inhabitants' sat down to a rather more sophisticated dinner.

After the eating a series of athletic matches were held as well as dancing to the three bands. The day ended with a grand firework display 'under the superintendence of Mr.Ellis chemist.' On this fiery note the victory celebrations ended - a day probably never to be forgotten by those who took part.
North Devon Journal 14.6.2001

46. The Indian Mutiny and North Devon

In the nineteenth century Britain spread its empire throughout the world by a mixture of trade and conquest. The jewel in the crown was India which had passed under the joint control of the Honourable East India Company and the British government. India was policed by the British Army which in 1857 mustered 40,000 men in the sub-continent, they being supported by a further 230,000 Indian troops - amongst whom discipline was variable.

In that year, however, the War Office in London issued new Enfield rifles to the Indian soldiers. The cartridges for these weapons had to be bitten before being inserted into the breech - and rumours began to fly that both pig and beef fat had been used to grease them. In actual fact it was the latter but the religious sensibilities of both Muslim and Hindu troops in the Indian regiments were offended.

On 10 May 1857 three regiments of local troops mutinied and marched on Delhi murdering any Europeans they met on the way. After a long bloody Summer order was restored though the final flames of the mutiny took many more months to totally extinguish - and how does this relate to North Devon? Well a fair number of the British troops came from Devon and although little was made of this at the time in May 1907 the *Journal* decided to mark the 50th anniversary of the uprising by interviewing four local survivors.

They began with Colonel Charles Yonge of Torrington who had been a lieutenant in the 16th Bombay Regiment in 1857. He had been stationed on the Western side of the sub-continent on the River Indus where he was in command of some 100 men who were 'almost entirely composed of what in those days were called Pandeys (another name for mutineers)'. His men actually remained loyal but local agitators kept turning up saying that a huge force of mutineers was coming to kill them. This unnerved Yonge's men and to keep order 'the informers were tied up, given three dozen lashes each' and kept in a lock-up until things quietened down.

On returning to his headquarters he had then to lead his unwilling men against some of their rioting fellows. He noted that though the 'whole regiment blazed away for upwards of two hours, only 15 of the rebels were killed.' After capturing and executing some of the mutineers the area became peaceful once more.

The *Journal* then moved on to record the memories of Sergeant T.Kingdom late of the 9th Lancers who had been born in Barnstaple. He reckoned 'There wasn't much that I missed in the Mutiny.' He had been at the siege of Delhi and had been chatting to a friend when a cannon ball took off his friend's leg. At another skirmish he speared a rebel cavalryman - and for his service was awarded 3 medals with 7 clasps - clearly a real veteran.

Corporal John Purchase late of the Shropshire Regiment was the next to be interviewed. Born in Barnstaple in 1824 to a shoemaker he and his 6 brothers all entered the Army with two of them dying in India. He enlisted into the 14th Foot in 1846 and served 9 years in the East Indies before going to India. During the Mutiny he was part of the column that relieved the siege of Lucknow when 'Forty miles we did without either bite or sup.' Unfortunately he received 'a nasty sabre cut' at Lucknow but went on to win 2 medals and 2 clasps and retire on an Army pension.

The fourth North Devonian to be featured was 82 year old H.Keene of Buckland Court near Bideford who had been an Indian District Superintendent in 1857. As soon as heard about the mutiny he raised new recruits to guard the town he governed. These groups of Europeans patrolled 'at unfixed hours' and 'kept the native police always on the alert'. He also printed his own money 'marked with a crest to prevent forgery.' Intriguingly Keene late became a Professor at Calcutta University and published several books on the mutiny.

Next year marks the 150th anniversary of the rising - but it is unlikely we will be recalling the event very much - it isn't one of the prouder moments in the history of the British Empire. It is, however, fascinating to think of North Devonians soldiering in the heat of India in the mid nineteenth century - so far from home in such an alien land.

North Devon Journal 2.3.2006

47. Let the French come!

In the late 1850s Britain became very uneasy about the military ambitions of Napoleon III of France. A wave of patriotic fervour swept the country and saw the establishment of numerous Volunteer Rifle Corps set up to defend their own local areas. Made up of local men every town in North Devon formed their own groups - each with its own distinctive uniform.

The Barnstaple Corps was known as the Sixth Devon Volunteer Rifles and in June 1860, on 'Waterloo Day', they staged their first public appearance in their new uniform. Numbering some 80 men and officers they collected in the Pannier Market at 3 p.m. under the command of Lt.Col.Wyllis 'who has served his country for more than a quarter of a century on the burning plains of India' - aided by Lieutenant Savile and Ensign Miller.

In addition to the riflemen there was an 18 strong band who though only having been practicing 6 weeks gave a 'performance' that was 'highly creditable to themselves'. The men were described as a fine body 'many of them nearly six feet in height, and vigorous and sinewy withal.' The *Journal* covered the occasion in massive detail lovingly describing the uniform, which was of a 'drab' colour ornamented with red and black braid. Buttons and belt clasps were electro-plated whilst the shako hat was of black leather with a silver star bearing the corps name - the whole being topped with a 'beautiful plume'.

Forming up behind their band the men marched around the town cheered by thousands of spectators. Stopping in front of the Guildhall the musicians struck up 'God Save the Queen' and three cheers were given for the Mayor. The men then marched on to Rackfield where for an hour they went through their paces 'marching and countermarching, running, skirmishing and silent firing' in front of a huge and appreciative audience. It was noted that 'not a man flinched or shewed signs of exhaustion.'

The troops then sat down to eat, the journalist noting rather oddly 'from the formation of the corps to the present moment there has been an entire absence of party feeling' in the formation. Party political squabbling was far more common in the nineteenth century than it is today and this particular comment is very revealing.

At 6 p.m. the whole corps sat down to dinner at the Fortescue Hotel where wine flowed and speeches went on for some time. Large numbers of toasts were given including the rather wordy 'The Queen, God bless her, and spare her for many years to enjoy the popularity which she had deservedly enjoyed ever since she ascended the throne of these realms.'

Henry Gribble the Mayor proposed a toast to the Volunteer movement reckoning them 'as a peace movement, inasmuch as the best security for peace was to show that we were prepared for war.' He noted that there were already 150,000 Riflemen in Britain - though he hoped this would soon double.

He was followed by various local notables also saying much the same thing in differing ways. Sir William Rae, for example, said that any French invading force would find 'every hedge, every ditch, would form a rampart, and those lined and bristling with the bayonets of 100,000 riflemen' - shades of Churchill?

After a rather extravagant number of toasts a martial song was sung, a fiery poem read out and the evening finally ended at midnight with all present ready to take the French on at a moment's notice!

North Devon Journal 27.2.2003

48. Two criminal Marines

The concept of the career criminal is often thought of as a modern one. The idea that people could spend their whole life in criminality is, however, nothing new - as a case in June 1861 shows. At the Barnstaple Quarter Sessions court two men, William Hill and James Scott, were charged with stealing 8 hens from Richard Packer. The court heard from P.c.George Jones that at 4 a.m. on the morning of Sunday 21st April he and P.c.Cawsey were on duty near a brickyard just past the Barbican area of Barnstaple.

They saw Hill and Scott walking along with the former having a bag over his shoulder. When they were some 15' from Trinity Street the police officers challenged them. Hill dropped the bag and 'threatened to knock my brains out' with a large stick he was carrying according to P.c.Jones' evidence. Hill then made his escape. Scott meanwhile picked up the bag and ran but was captured by P.c.Cawsey. Looking into the bag the policemen found 2 headless chickens and 6 with heads - which were then identified by John Ridge who worked for Richard Packer. The policemen put Scott in the cells and then went looking for Hill who they found and arrested 3 hours later. The magistrates hearing the case immediately found the pair guilty and then asked for evidence of previous convictions. The list that was then read out was startling.

A letter from the Royal Marine Barracks in Plymouth recorded that Scott and Hill had both been in the Marines but had been discharged with their papers bearing the comment 'Worthless Character'. Whilst in the Marines Scott had been gaoled three times in Jamaica and had been court martialled four times! He had also been gaoled twice in 1856 in the Navy prison at Devonport for assaulting the police. Whilst in Barnstaple as a civilian he had been arrested six times for attacking the police, for being drunk, for theft and even 'indecently exposing his person.'

His partner in crime Hill had an even longer listing of wrongdoing. Whilst in the Marines he had been court martialled twice and spent four terms in gaol on bread and water including 3 days 'in the dark cells' which were for the punishment of the most recalcitrant prisoners. After being discharged he returned to Barnstaple and according to Superintendent Moran of the borough police 'has been a pest to the inhabitants.' He had been gaoled three times for theft, three times for assault on townspeople and four times for assaulting the police, twice for indecent exposure and once for being drunk and disorderly.

The Governor of Devonport prison wrote in a letter 'I know them both well, having had them in my custody several times; and I candidly confess to you that I never heard worse language from any prisoner, or had to deal with more violent characters than they were.'

Superintendent Moran reckoned 'the two prisoners have been linked together in crime from they very boyhood up to the present time.' Clearly they were not model citizens! It is no surprise therefore to find the Barnstaple court after hearing this catalogue of criminal activities handing out severe punishments to the two. Hill was sentenced to 'penal servitude' for 4 years and Scott to gaol 'with hard labour' for 8 months. Doubtless the townsfolk of Barnstaple slept more soundly in their beds following the removal of these two characters.

North Devon Journal 20.3.2003

49. Preparing for the Nazi invasion

The Second World War began in 1939 yet for the first 7 months or so nothing much happened - the so-called 'Phoney War' period. This lasted until April 1940 when the retreat from Europe and the Dunkirk episode suggested for the first time that the invasion of Britain might become a deadly possibility. To meet this eventuality the Home Guard was formed and Invasion Committees were set up to plan for the unthinkable. The minutes of the Bideford Committee have survived and are now kept in the North Devon Record Office where they make fascinating reading.

The first meeting dates from 21 August 1941 when an impressive body of councillors and service personnel met to plan out their work. Thus Mrs.McHale, the 'Food Executive Officer' agreed to carry out a survey of supplies in the town whilst Dr.Pearson was to report on the arrangements to deal with casualties, water supply and sanitation in emergencies. The grandly named 'Local Fuel Overseer' was to detail supplies of oil and paraffin whilst letters were sent to local Boy Scout troops, the Cycling Club and the Pigeon Fanciers Society 'with regard to arrangements for emergency communications.'

Meeting again a week later the Committee heard that all the cyclists were in the Home Guard or other services and the best the Club could do was to offer 'a number of female members'. Their numbers were deemed insufficient and the Committee decided that local Head Teachers should be asked 'if they have any scholars over 13 willing to act as Cycle Messengers.' They would supplement the carrier pigeons already organised by the Home Guard.

In fact some 61 boys and girls were enrolled into the Bideford Messenger Corps 'all with parents' permission' and they wore 'distinctive Armlets' provided by the Women's Voluntary Service (do any of these armlets survive?).

In September the Committee agreed that 'the public be taken into confidence and educated with a view to co-operation particularly in the provision of beds, bedding etc for casualties.' This material was to go to Geneva School which 'had been earmarked as a Shadow Hospital' by the Ministry of Health.

More importantly 'in the event of the emergency visualised developing [i.e. the invasion] all able bodied men and women, except those already engaged on essential services' were to be requested to report to the town's Labour Exchange. This would follow public announcements 'made by loud speaker van, if available'. Rather oddly the Committee also agreed 'That a supply of posters be printed and kept in reserve to make such announcement, should the loud speaker be not available' (again, do any survive').

The Committee next turned their attention to Bideford Bridge and its possible destruction by bombing. Admiral Franklin, then in charge of the estuary, agreed to provide barges if a ferry service was needed. The Committee for its part agreed to build a landing stage outside Tanton's Hotel.

On the 18th of September a 'gas exercise' was carried out in the town with tear gas being used to simulate the expected poison gas. Two members of the local ARP (Air Raid Precautions) W.Broad and L.Jackson were in charge of this. Also in September Edgehill College was designated as another emergency hospital as was Bideford Grammar School in October.

The final entries for 1941 record the preparation of a report on the availability of local cranes and tractors to move heavy weights. That these weren't adequate is shown when it was noted that the public were to be asked to help the Home Guard to put road blocks in place 'when required.'

The minutes extend for some years after this but just this brief look shows how local people responded to the threat of invasion - although, if one were being truthful, we can only be thankful that the Nazis didn't come. Indeed I suspect that such local committees were more about sustaining morale rather than repelling invaders.

North Devon Journal 14.10.2004

RELIGION

50. The wisdom of age

If we could travel back in time to the distant past one thing would strike us very quickly - the absence of paperwork and forms. Most of our ancestors before the mid-nineteenth century would have been functionally illiterate and the government ran without today's obsessive need for records and documentation. If a record was needed then appeal had to be made to peoples' memories.

One aspect of life that relied heavily on these memories was the tithe system. Up until the last century every property owner had to pay a certain sum, the tithe or tenth, either in money or goods to the church. Disputes were common as is shown by one from Frithelstock in 1577.

John Frayne who lived at a farm called 'Mylford' reckoned that he was being overcharged on his tithe dues and had refused to pay them - thus explaining his appearance in court to fight his case. Three of the oldest parishioners were summoned to the court to give the judge the benefit of their memories.

The first to speak was John Williams aged 74, a lifelong resident of Frithelstock. About 40 years before he had been one of the parish churchwardens charged with collecting the tithes. The owner of 'Mylford' at that date was a certain John Liteljohn who actually lived in nearby Buckland Brewer. The two churchwardens had called on him and received the tithe payment of one bushel of oats worth 5p and one peck of wheat worth 4p.

His evidence was followed by that of William Small aged 87 who must have been one of the oldest North Devonians alive in that era of short lifespans. The court record suggests that William must have been bed-bound and that he had only come to court at the request of the previous witness who had been his fellow-churchwarden. His memory of events was the same as Williams' though he did add, as if to bolster it, that 'he ys not payd nor p(ro)mysed Any thynge for his Laboure' and 'that he beareth no males to John ffrayne nor to his knowledge he ded never se hym before this daye.'

ELIZA HONEY

BEGS to call attention to her well-assorted Stock of General

STATIONERY,

Comprising Letter and Note Papers, Envelopes
Pens, Quills, Pencils, Ledgers, Day Books,
Cash Books, Metallics, Memorandums,
Pass Books, &c.

PRINTING

Tables, Catalogues, Circulars, Cards, Invoice
Book Work, Rules, Pamphlets,
Handbills, Placards,

Can be produced at the shortest notice, and on
the most reasonable terms

MATHEMATICAL INSTRUMENTS, &c.

PIANOS, HARMONIUMS,

BIBLES, PRAYER BOOKS,
CHURCH SERVICES.

Card Boards, Milled Boards, &c.

Portfolios, Writing, Music, and Sermon Cases
Made to Order and Repaired.

POPULAR PUBLICATIONS OF THE DAY

BOOKS & PERIODICALS TO ORDER

Publications of the Religious Tract Society.

LONDON DAILY & WEEKLY
NEWSPAPERS
SUPPLIED.

LADIES' LEATHER BAGS,
BOYS' SCHOOL BAGS, &c

PATENT MEDICINE DEPOT.

*An advertisement showing the range of goods and services offered by
Eliza Honey at The Bideford Gazette Offices in Grenville Street following
the death of her husband Thomas in 1856 (see article no. 98)*

BIDEFORD, NORTH DEVON.

TO BE SOLD, by Public Auction, by Mr. FREDERICK LEE, at Maunder's 'Newfoundland Inn,' on Thursday, the 24th day of April instant, at 6 o'clock in the evening (if not previously disposed of by Private Contract, of which, due Notice will be given), the Fee-Simple and Inheritance of and in all that

DWELLING HOUSE AND BUSINESS PREMISES,

Situate in Grenville-street, in the Town aforesaid, now and for many years past in the occupation of Mrs. HONEY.

The House contains on the Ground Floor, Spacious Front Shop, with Two Windows, Parlour, Kitchen, Wash House, Offices, Court Yard, &c.; First Floor, a Large Sitting Room, Bed Room, and Linen Closet; Second Floor, Four Good Bedrooms, with Attic over. Leading from the Front Shop, and approached by Stairs is a Printing Office.

The Premises are well supplied with Hard and Soft Water, and conveniently fitted up with Cupboards, Grates, and Chimney Pieces.

The above offers an excellent opportunity to parties requiring a good Business Premises, being contiguous to the Market and principal thoroughfare in the Town, and for the past 50 years has been known (and occupied) as a Printing and Bookselling House.

For further particulars, apply at the Office of the Auctioneer, or to Mr. ROOKER, Solicitor, *Bideford.*

Dated April 2nd, 1862. [5411

In April 1862 the premises of Eliza Honey were offered for sale

Above: The Chapel of St Anne's in the centre of Barnstaple is seen here in a very early photograph - with grave-stones still surrounding it well before they were 'tidied up'. The graveyard was closed following a Government inspector's report on its unsavoury condition in 1849.

Caen Street in Braunton about 1925 - with just one car in the road and no TV aerials - with cider at a very reasonable 9d (4p) a quart (2 pints).

Above: Some of Sir Oswald Mosley's fascist 'Blackshirts' are seen here at Stoney Cross near Bideford in 1933 (see article No 95).

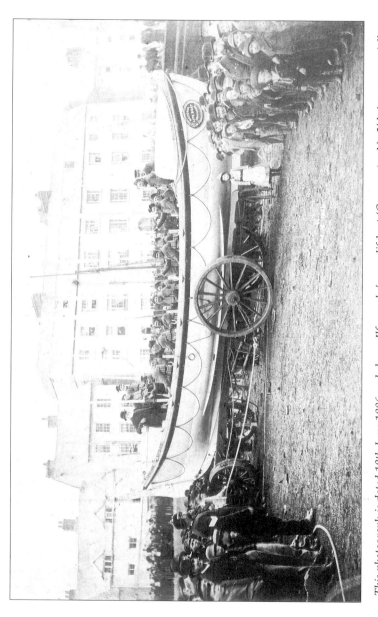

This photograph is dated 18th June 1886 and shows Ilfracombe's new lifeboat 'Co-operator No 2' being ceremonially handed over to the National Lifeboat Institution. The boat was the gift of the Central Co-operative Board in Manchester and it stayed at this station until 1893.

Torrington May Fair is one of the most notable events in the North Devon Calendar, and here we see the crowd dancing in the square in 1952

The opening of Barnstaple Fair around 1910 with the men of the Barnstaple Fire Brigade leading the Mayor's party.

The final witness was Patrick Cudmore, aged 62, who had spent 34 years living in Frithelstock. He had been churchwarden along with Stephen Palmer, seven or eight years previously. On taking the job they had been 'Instructed by the old men of the p(ar)yshe' what sums were due from which properties for tithe payments. When he had gone to Frayne's house he was given some oats and wheat but 'the old men sayd (this) was not his full due because yt ded lacke some what of the full measure.'

The documents that record this fascinating example of oral history do not unfortunately tell us what the result of this case was. We can, however, be fairly certain that Frayne lost as the evidence of the three old men would have been the deciding factor.

In cases such as this the accused had three choices. He could attempt to find other elderly parishioners whose memories suited his case, he could pay up gracefully or he could refuse to pay. If he chose the latter the church (which of course controlled the tithe system) could excommunicate him or exclude him from church life - including the rites of baptism, marriage and burial. If the excommunicant continued his opposition the parish priest could order all of his congregation i.e. the whole village, to have no dealings with him whatsoever in any way - a punishment to be greatly feared in that period of isolated village communities. I think we can assume Frayne paid up - less than willingly almost certainly but old men's memories and precedent were powerful enemies to take on.

North Devon Journal 1.10.1998

51. When the vestry ran Ilfracombe

The local government system we have today where councils are elected and are answerable to the electorate only dates from the 1830s. Prior to that date many functions we expect councils to do today were carried out by the vestry. This was a self-selected group made up of the 'principal inhabitants' of the parish (usually the richest) who met in the church vestry to govern much of the life of their community.

One such existed in Ilfracombe and luckily its records, in the form of a volume of minutes, have survived from the years 1740 to 1813. It consists of a long thin book covered in parchment (and sellotape!) and is written in a variety of cramped and hard-to-read hands. If, however, one perseveres the book reveals many aspects of the town's history over these years.

In May 1740, for example, the vestry members set the expenses allowed to the parish constable at 5/- (25p) per year 'and no more'. This poorly remunerated position was filled annually by ballot or under a rota system and was not a sought after job in those days before the existence of a professional police force.

Several other references to law keeping occur in the minutes. In 1746 it was decided to pay 1/- (5p) per day and the same per night 'to a Guardsman for watching'. This was presumably a town watchman rather than a coastguard as the latter service was under the control of the Royal Navy. A note adds that if the same person watched both day and night they were only to receive 1/6 (7.5p) presumably on the basis that they would be too exhausted to be of much value unlike a fresh man each shift!

Five years later the meeting warned that if any publicans provided accommodation to 'Runners or Strollers' (tramps) they would be responsible for them if they fell ill - the vestry would not cough up any public money for them.

In 1770 the minutes record that the vestry agreed to pay the prosecution costs involved in a theft case involving Elizabeth Downe, the wife of Edward, and 'some or one of his Daughters'. A shift or petticoat had been stolen from a widow called Jane Rodd and she had later found it, washed and hung out to dry, on the 'Garden Hedge' of the Downe family. Presumably Widow Rodd would not have been able to afford to take the case to court unless her costs were covered.

A year earlier the vestry became involved in what we would term pre-emptive action against crime when they had agreed to have a wall built around 'the Waste' in front of the Church House - the earliest form of workhouse in Ilfracombe. This was to be constructed by the inmates 'as it would be a means of keeping several People to work (who it is well known are accustomed to be rambling abroad and to be absent from the House when they ought to be at home and following their Labour).' Job creation schemes it seems are nothing new.

The Church House appears often in these records sometimes being called the workhouse or poor house. In 1761 Geoffery Davis was elected Governor of the workhouse at a salary of £8 per year which included drawing up the accounts of 'necessaries bought' and 'work done'. This latter is a reference to the income produced from the labour of the inmates which could include spinning of wool and the unpicking of old tarred rope (oakum) which was then used to caulk ships.

Sixteen years later George Dyer and his wife Mary became the new Master and Mistress of the workhouse though their salary by then had been reduced to just £5 per year. Evidently Dyer didn't think much of this and in 1783 James Dunford and his wife took over the position. By 1785 their wages had been raised to £13 but in that year the vestry decided 'that the Governors Salary of Thirteen Pounds a year is rather more than the Parish can well afford to give' and reduced it down to £5 again.

The Dunfords seem to have left in disgust and one Peter Furze was appointed but only a few months later 'was turn'd out of being Governor for disobedience' and William Smith put in his place - at a salary of £7. Clearly the vestry had problems with its employees.

In 1769 the minutes record an agreement between Christopher Bowen, one of the Overseers of the Poor, with Richard Lawrence to take George Bowen a 'Poor Boy' from the workhouse and employ him as a servant at the princely wage of £1 per year. The vestry were happy to support this example of virtual slavery as it meant one less pauper's mouth to feed and thus a saving on the rates.

These poor children ended up in the workhouse either when orphaned or when their unmarried mother couldn't afford to support them. In this latter case the vestry made sure that the fathers paid their share of the child's upkeep. In September 1778 for example William Hopkins agreed to pay the then large sum of £12.10.0 (£12.50) towards the cost of bringing up the illegitimate child he had fathered on Mary Smith though this would be returned if the child died in the three years following its birth. The Ilfracombe parish registers reveals that his daughter Mary was baptised on 27 December 1778 whilst there is no entry of her burial for the three years in question.

A similar agreement was reached between John Rowe over his child being carried by Elizabeth Braily in 1799 although in this case he was only charged £10.10.0 (£10.50) presumably because he was poorer than Hopkins.

Another important part of the vestry's work was to do with medical care for the poor. In 1740 for example John Clark was appointed as 'Apothecary and Chirurgeon' (surgeon) to the paupers in the workhouse for £2 a year - an appointment repeated many times and with many different medical men over the entire run of the minutes book.

Occasionally serious cases which cost a lot more were presented to the vestry members for their agreement as to the charges. In June 1752 it was recorded how John Clark 'propos'd to undertake to cut off William Hughs' Leg and to be paid for his Trouble provided he makes a Cure the Sum of Twelve Pounds & twelve shillings' (£12.60). Interestingly it was also noted that if Hughs 'should happen to die, occasion'd by the Operation the Said Mr John Clark to be paid for his Trouble Two Pounds & Two Shillings' (£2.10). Payment by results obviously - although if his patient died Clark was to be allowed the costs of the bandages used! The burial registers show that a William Hughs was buried in January 1754 so presumably if this is the same man the operation was successful - at least in the short term.

In 1760 John Clark agreed to attempt a cure of Mary Richard's breast which seems to have been cancerous. If successful he was to receive 4 guineas (£4.20) and if not then just half that sum. His treatment involved amputation and happily a search of the burial register for the ensuing five years shows no entry for Mary so perhaps she survived? - no mean feat in those days before anaesthetics. Six years later Clark amputated John Thomas's leg for a payment of 8 guineas (£8.40) and again his patient seems to have survived - all of which suggests that Clark was a very proficient surgeon.

When a pauper did die, however, the vestry paid for the coffin and there are many references to contracts with carpenters for their production. In 1768 Samuel Cross was being paid 5/- (25p) for each 'Parish Coffin' and this slowly rose to 10/6 (52.5p) by 1813 when John Berry was supplying them.

If the poor were lucky they could be educated with the help of 'Madam Pincombe's Endowment' which was a charitable fund set up by this public minded lady whose money paid for both the teachers and the scholars' fees. Her money also provided a pension of £2 per year to paupers chosen by the vestry.

Not just crime and the poor were looked after by the vestry. In 1772 they hired Thomas Smith of Countisbury to tackle a plague of foxes. In 1795 they were offering a bounty of 15 guineas (£15.75) to any man who volunteered to serve in the Royal Navy and help Nelson take on Napoleon's fleet. On many occasions they paid for the repair of roads within the parish as in 1759 when they had 'the remainder of the Cawsey (causeway) against Lower Bowden in Barnstaple Road' paved at the very odd cost of 1 5/8d per square yard.

Perhaps the strangest entry occurs in November 1757 when the vestry took out a summons against 'the Masters of the Pilot Boats and other principal Persons concern'd' to claim the costs of £10 per day incurred by the treatment required by 200 men landed from a French ship who were suffering from 'an Infectious fever'. Presumably quarantine laws had not been followed and the vestry saw no reason why they should pay.

Hopefully from this article one can see what a treasure house of historical material can be found in the minute book of the old vestry - indeed one might say all human life is contained in its pages.

North Devon Journal 11.3.1999 + 18.3.1999

52. The floating shroud

Some years ago St.Mary Magdalene's church in Barnstaple was demolished. All that is left today is its graveyard, with an entrance from Bear Street, in which the gravestones have been neatly stacked around the walls. Some 150 years ago this quiet graveyard was the centre of a painful scandal as we shall see.

The history of the church itself goes back to 1824 when a committee was set up to establish a second church in Barnstaple which, at that date, had only one church and more importantly, only one Church of England graveyard. Nothing came of this until 1842 when a public meeting was held in the Guildhall where those attending decided to go ahead with construction. This move was helped by the offer of £2000 from the Reverend John Scott who was just about to become curate at Pilton.

The church was designed to hold 1200 and the work was entrusted to a committee led by three men - the Reverend Henry Luxmoore of St.Peter's, Gilbert Knill Cotton the Town Mayor and William Snow, a local headmaster. During the building phase the committee met on 77 occasions, a huge number of times but necessary as the original plans were shelved at one point, work began at one site and was then abandoned and the Reverend Scott suddenly withdrew his offer and went off in a huff (later to return to Barnstaple, build Holy Trinity church and install himself as vicar!)

Notwithstanding these setbacks the committee purchased a suitable plot of land off Bear Street for £500. This housed a variety of land uses including a saw pit, a tanyard and a well which were all filled in before building began - a move that came to haunt the committee later. The siting was deliberately chosen to serve the many poor people living in the Derby area of the town who were virtually excluded from St.Peter's where most of the pews were rented by the rich.

The foundation stone was laid in October 1844 and two years later, in November 1846, the church was consecrated by the Bishop of Exeter. The first incumbent was the Reverend James Pycroft who seems to have spent more time writing about cricket than serving his parishioners. Indeed it was noted of him that 'he was not often to be seen in his parish and disliked visiting the poor or the sick, having a wholesome dread of dirt and disease.'

If he did not serve his flock that well at least the graveyard attached to the church met a long-felt need for extra burial space in the town. St.Peter's churchyard was so full that coffins were being buried very near the surface. Sadly the presence of the old tan pits made itself all too obvious in November 1856 when the

Journal carried an eye-witness account 'of a most revolting scene' that took place in the new graveyard.

John Nott, a retired shipwright and inmate of Barnstaple Workhouse, had died and was to be buried in a grave on the eastern side of the church. This area was known to be 'swampy' and was thus reserved for paupers and 'afternoon funerals' (when the poor buried their dead). Any grave excavated in this part of the churchyard was immediately half filled with water - which even three hours of bailing could not empty.

The *Journal* report is worth quoting in full at this point, 'in a few minutes the mourners had arrived with the corpse, which floated on its being lowered into the grave, and it required that a person should steady it with a shovel while the clergyman was reading the service for the dead.' The reporter added 'A more disgusting sight can scarcely be conceived.' It is interesting to note that there is no reference to a coffin - presumably Workhouse inmates weren't considered worth the expense.

The *Journal* fulminated against this state of affairs but as burial in the churchyard was far cheaper than in the then recently opened Borough Cemetery the poor continued to choose graves in the former. Indeed burials continued up until 1903 by which time St.Mary Magdalene's churchyard was becoming as crowded as St.Peter's had been 50 years before.

Today the site is a quiet oasis amid the bustle of 21st century Barnstaple - worth visiting to see the remaining gravestones, mute witnesses to the final sad events in our ancestors' lives.
North Devon Journal 6.9.2001

53. Richard Blackmore and beef

Richard Blackmore is one of North Devon's most famous writers. Author of '*Lorna Doone*' and many other works his family were spread widely in North Devon. His uncle, also named Richard, was the rector of Charles near Brayford in the second half of the nineteenth century. It was in this role rather than as uncle to the world famous writer that he appeared in the *Journal*'s letter columns in 1867.

The rector had put pen to paper following a run-of-the-mill report on the charitable distribution of beef to the poor of Charles at the National School Room in the village. The reporter had noted, in passing, that the school had been 'erected by the munificence of the landlords and farmers' of the parish in the year 1859.

Blackmore wrote in to say this was not true, indeed the 'landlords and farmers' had only provided 'a few days' cartage of materials' - which he sarcastically added was 'a great help!' In actual fact the school had been built using three 'liberal and handsome donations' from Earl Fortescue, John Fortescue and Sir Peregrine Acland along with a grant from the government. Even this wasn't enough and a debt of £200 'devolved on me'. This was because the school was a church maintained one and Blackmore as the local representative of the church became personally liable. The 'children's pence' and an annual government grant never covered this debt which Blackmore had to service every year.

The rector went on to point out that he and two friends paid for the 'fine heifer' whose flesh was distributed amongst the parish poor - nothing had come from the local 'landlords and farmers' although the heifer's owner Mr.Wedlake did sell it to them at less than the market price. In a postscript Blackmore made the point that he had no part in the distribution which, according to village gossip, had been very unfair.

The following week, as might have been expected, the *Journal* carried a reply from William Huxtable of Brayford Hill who pointed out that Blackmore had been very grateful for the 'cartage' help when the school was being built. Additionally the £200 debt fell to just £17 when one subtracted the expenses Blackmore claimed for himself! As to the distribution of beef Huxtable claimed the rector had been clearly involved in the choice of the recipients - many of whom were his 'favourites who live in proximity to the church.' Such an accusation was a gift to the *Journal* which was a solidly non-conformist supporting newspaper!

Needless to say Blackmore replied in the next week's edition of the *Journal* pointing out he disputed Huxtable's claims over the debt and noting that he had invited him to see the account books for the school at the Rectory but Huxtable hadn't bothered to come and see them. As to the fairness or otherwise of the beef distribution he could only add that 'rib beef' and 'the other best pieces' had all gone to young and middle-aged men and women who were employed - 'to the old and infirm were given the coarsest and bony pieces' which might strike us as slightly odd today.

The next week another letter attacking Blackmore was published but the *Journal*'s editor had evidently had enough writing that the 'correspondence must cease'. With that the story died away but what a fascinating window on the past this exchange of letters provides.

54. A grave charge of vandalism
Vandalism seems to be so common today that we think of it as being a curse of our age. Hardly a week goes by without reports of mindless damage from every part of North Devon. Such behaviour is not, however, just associated with the late twentieth century. Over 120 years ago there was an astonishing, not to say bizarre, case from Westdown on the Barnstaple to Ilfracombe road. The vandal in this case was one Samuel Giffard and his target was a tomb in the local churchyard - which hardly chimes with today's view of Victorian respect for the dead!

In December 1875 P.c.Joseph Sanders was on duty about 11 p.m. in Westdown. Walking between the village and the Foxhunters Inn he encountered Giffard 'carrying a lot of iron railings and some iron bars.' Not surprisingly he asked what Giffard was doing with them and was told it was just some old iron purchased from the local blacksmith. The constable knew that Giffard had indeed bought iron like this before and so went on his way.

It was only later that he realised where the iron had come from and went to arrest Giffard. This wasn't too easy as his suspect was 'armed with an iron bar, and made great resistance and was a very powerful man.' Eventually, and with some assistance Giffard was carted off to gaol where he told the police in which field he had dumped the iron rails. P.c.Sanders recovered the material and took it to Westdown churchyard where it had clearly been removed from a tomb of the Symons family.

At the trial William Reed of Braunton, who acted as agent to the Symons family, gave evidence as to recognizing the iron work adding that no orders had been issued, or even considered, about having it removed from the grave. He set a value on the stolen ironwork of 5/- (25p).

Giffard's own evidence consisted of an account of his actions and a straight- forward admission of guilt. On the day in question he had been to church then gone to the pub and, being told that the railings were due for removal, made his unsteady way to the churchyard where, with the help of an iron bar, he had broken the railings from the grave and then, after encountering the policeman, dumped them in a nearby field.

The only reason he suggested as to why he carried out this act of vandalism was that he 'had heard that the railing was objected to as dissightly [sic] and was to be removed, and he had obeyed a mad impulse to show by use of his iron bar and by his great muscular strength how easily it could be done.' Clearly vandals were as daft then as they are today.

His lawyer then entered a plea for leniency on his client's behalf claiming, outrageously, that as Giffard had thrown the ironwork away he clearly hadn't stolen it! He also added that Giffard would pay whatever costs were required to reinstate the grave to its former condition. It was also pointed out that not only was Giffard the son of a clergyman but he was also a 'man of education and of very good parts, in proof of which his advocate produced a letter he had addressed to a local paper which showed much ability' - an interesting piece of evidence to prove sanity!

The magistrates listened to this along with Giffard's open admittance of guilt and, reckoning the case to be 'almost identical with that of sacrilege', sentenced him to two months imprisonment. So next time you read in the *Journal* of modern vandals and begin blaming modern day youths just remember that such behaviour is nothing new.

North Devon Journal 10.6.1999

55. Religious passions in Torrington

It is difficult for us today as we enter the 21st century to realise the level of passions aroused in the 19th century by the split in the Church of England between 'high' and 'low' churchmen. Its roots are tangled and not that easy to follow but, suffice to say, the 'high' church tended to accept elements of ritual, often identified with Catholics, in religious services, whilst those in the 'low' church shunned all such ideas identifying them as 'papist' and 'foreign'. Needless to say when 'low' church congregations were sent 'high' church clergy sparks flew - and no more so than in Torrington.

The town, of course, has always had a somewhat stormy religious history but in 1878 the flare-up was centred on a small brass cross some fifteen inches high. In March of that year the curate the Reverend H.O.Francis brought the brass cross from London and the vicar and he decided to place it on the reredos over the altar in St.Michael's church in Torrington.

Such a seemingly innocuous ornament was seen as an 'objectionable Romish relic' by the parish churchwarden John Lake who promptly took it down although he did leave two nearby flower vases in place on the grounds that he thought 'they can do no harm'. This action seems somewhat bizarre to us but a contemporary report on the case noted that Lake had 'become so disgusted with the present state of things connected with church matters that he has made up his mind to retire from the office at Easter.' Clearly other things had been going on here but what they were is left unsaid.

The reporter in this instance strikes one as being very biased when we read that 'it is hoped the parishioners will look out for a suitable successor, who will not fear to speak out his mind, and counteract, as far as possible, the introduction of semi-popish performances etc.' Clearly the writer was not a 'high' church supporter.

Within a fortnight, however, events had moved on. A new white cross appeared on the altar - but in the form of an embroidered one the altar cloth. This was reckoned to be 'the handiwork of some ladies closely connected with the vicar or curate.' The churchwarden may have been thwarted but it was noted that Reverend Mr.Francis the curate was shortly to leave Torrington.

In a very uncharitable remark the then reporter for the *Journal* in Torrington wrote that 'Considering how the church people have been divided and scattered since his appointment to this place, the sooner he leaves the better it will be for all concerned.' Victorian writers didn't mince their words! Indeed the anonymous writer went on to note that subscriptions to various church bodies and appeals had 'recently very much fallen off' the clear implication being that the actions of the Reverend Mr.Francis were behind this fall in support.

In the event churchwarden Lake did resign and in May 1878 the Bishop of Exeter, Dr.Temple, came to Torrington to hold a conference with the clergy of the area. Whilst there he also held a confirmation service at which those locals who attended 'were not a little surprised to find that the brass cross, the subject of so much earlier dispute, was back in its previous position near the altar.'

It seems that the vicar and his curate had ensured the appointment of a new churchwarden who was more amenable to their view of church worship. Additionally they appear to have obtained the tacit support of the Bishop to defeat the 'low' church adherents in their congregation.

A clever move and one that seems very strange to us today in the light of the decline in such passionately held religious beliefs since then. Interestingly the Reverend Mr.Francis did not win in the long term as within a year he was at the centre of a massive scandal engineered by his enemies - but I will leave that for a later article.

North Devon Journal 5.8.1999

56. The clerical sex scandal in Torrington

A little time ago I wrote about the dispute that hit Torrington in 1878 between 'high' and 'low' churchmen. The winner on that occasion was the Reverend H.Francis the 'high' church curate of St.Michael's church. His triumph was short lived as in 1879 he became the victim of a sexual scandal which made the headlines.

It began innocuously enough when the married clergyman was walking on Torrington Commons near the cemetery and met a Miss Lucy Jones. After a few minute's conversation they parted whereupon William Balkwell a young labourer of Torrington came up to her and alleged he had seen the two 'sitting on the ground' in each other's arms for half an hour. She called the Reverend Francis back and Balkwell repeated his allegation adding that he would keep quiet for 10/- (50p) 'hush money'. Bizarrely, in the light of later denials of impropriety, Francis paid him. Unfortunately Balkwell didn't keep his part of the bargain and rumours quickly swept the town being exaggerated at each step - probably helped on their way by the many enemies Francis had made in his earlier battle.

In the event things got so bad that Francis had his blackmailer summonsed and the initial hearing came before the local court in September 1879. Here the two opposing stories were gone through. Both the clergyman and Lucy Jones (described as 'a lady of some personal attractions') denied any wrongdoing though they did admit their chance meeting had occurred in a small secluded hollow - but had only lasted 5-6 minutes. When asked if she had used her umbrella 'to conceal yourself from observation' Lucy denied it vehemently. In his defence Balkwell said that Francis had offered him the money to keep quiet - he hadn't asked for it at all. Bearing in mind he was facing 3 years of 'penal servitude' if found guilty this statement isn't surprising.

After considering the evidence the magistrates decided there was no case to answer and dismissed Balkwell. The reporter covering the case noted that 'from the demeanour of the public it was easy enough to see that the decision was one of which they approved' - indeed Balkwell's costs were paid by 'a public subscription.'

A few days later the humiliated clergyman sent a circular leaflet to 'the principal inhabitants' of Torrington reproducing the Bishop of Exeter's letter of support and adding the comment 'Trusting that what has satisfied the Bishop will also satisfy you.' Unfortunately at the same time the Torrington Board of

Guardians met and voted to ask Francis to resign his post of chaplain to the local workhouse.

The beleaguered curate ignored this vote and turned up the next Sunday to take the workhouse service as usual but the Chairman of the Board ordered that the chapel doors be locked and the curate returned home defeated. Another leaflet in support of the couple was then circulated around Torrington which reckoned that Balkwell was 'a member of the criminal class'. The *Journal* editor who reprinted this leaflet also thought Balkwell a 'worthless character' but considered Francis had been stupid to pay any money to him.

On November 5th effigies of Francis and Jones were burnt instead of the traditional Guy Fawkes. Henry Pope, a train driver, was reported to his bosses for collecting money for the construction of the effigies from passengers at Torrington station - whilst the actual burning attracted a crowd of 2000 people!

Within a fortnight a Government Inspector came to Torrington to hold an inquiry into the legality of Francis' suspension from his workhouse post. All the evidence was gone through again though this time witnesses came forward to say they had often seen Francis and Jones together both on the Commons and at various other places including Bideford, Barnstaple and Exeter.

The Inspector, somewhat surprisingly in the light of this evidence, found no reason for Francis to give up his workhouse post but, finding his position untenable, the curate resigned his position and indeed decided to leave Torrington altogether. At his leaving his friends presented him with £21, a hymn book and a testimonial address signed by 300 people. Mrs.Francis was given 'a very handsome photograph album'. With this the victory of the 'low' church over their 'high' church enemy was complete and so Torrington settled down - at least until the next outbreak of religious sectarianism.

North Devon Journal 6.1.2000

57. The Sally Army meets the yobs of Torrington
An unusual court case heard in Torrington in September 1884 began with a lawyer stating that 'the presence of the Salvation

Army in any town was not by any means an unmixed blessing.' This unexpected statement introduced a complicated case of summons and cross-summons between members of the 'Army' and inhabitants of Torrington described as 'the rough element.'

The 'Army' had been undertaking a series of processions through the town singing well-known but usually staid hymns to rousing marching tunes such as 'Johnny comes marching home'. Needless to say these attracted large crowds and on this occasion it was claimed that a boy called Short accidentally bumped into one of the Salvationists - James Gilbert.

James was wearing 'an article of dress on which the words 'Christ for me' appeared' but unfortunately he didn't seem to accept the Christian ethos of 'turning the other cheek' as, it was alleged, that he proceeded to push the boy to the ground and rub his face in the mud!

Some bystanders, including a confusingly named John Gilbert, considered this excessive and rushed to the boy's aid. James, however, took his belt off 'twisted it round his wrist' and began swinging it round until he hit John's hand. The belt was produced in court and the prosecuting lawyer pointed out the heavy clasp which he thought only 'a dangerous lunatic' would use as it was 'a fearsome' weapon.

James claimed in his defence that he had only used the belt to defend himself against some aggressive men. In fact he had summonsed John along with John Short, Henry Cawsey, George Sage, Richard Ward and Charles Norman for assaulting him.

James then gave his version of events. He had been marching with the Salvationists when, near the Baptist chapel, the boy Short kept pushing against him. He didn't push him over but merely 'put his hand on his shoulder and requested him to go away.' John Gilbert then gave James 'a blow' and John along with five of his friends 'made a rush upon him.' In self-defence he took off his belt shouting 'Back, or I will use my buckle' though he swore he hadn't actually used it, rather he was overwhelmed and kicked to the ground. At one point he heard someone call out 'Now let us take him to the pavement and dash his brains out' - presumably he was in the road which at that date would not have been surfaced with tarmac. Only the arrival of his fellow Salvationists saved him from possible severe injury.

Faced with such directly conflicting accounts the magistrates withdrew to discuss the case privately. At the end of their deliberations they decided to fine all the 'roughs' 25p each noting that the Salvationists 'were entitled to protection so long as they marched in order and in a proper manner.' They also reprimanded James saying he had 'acted unwisely and prematurely in taking off his belt at the time he did' and this could only have 'excited the crowd.'

The report of the case, which lasted 7 hours, notes that large numbers of spectators were in court and as the Salvationsits left 'in a body' they were 'loudly booed by the assembled crowd whose sympathies were evidently with the persons who had been fined.'

So ended this particular incident but many others occurred in these early years of the 'Army's' history. Who, though, could imagine a similar scene today when polite indifference and even embarrassment seems to meet religious enthusiasts who try to publicly proclaim their faith?

58. Open air religion and violence

Our ancestors took their religion more seriously than we do today - to the extent that religious meetings and disputes could well end up in court. In May 1906 the magistrates at Barnstaple heard an assault case which arose directly from the visit of some 'Wickliffe Preachers'. These odd sounding people promoted a fairly unusual view of religious dogma and tended to gather volatile crowds wherever they went.

The first case saw John Neill, a young man, charged with assaulting John Pidgeon outside Queen Anne's Walk where the visiting preachers were holding an open air meeting. Pidgeon, who worked at Dornat & Co's Mineral Water Works, had been in the crowd listening to the service when Neill ran amongst the assembled people throwing liquid around from a bottle he was carrying. Some of it hit Pidgeon's face and he experienced a burning sensation whilst Neill ran off.

Meeting him later he demanded to know what the liquid had been as he himself thought it was acid. Neill denied this saying 'Something I have bought at the chemist's. It would not hurt anybody.' He went on to claim it was just to produce a smell.

The prosecuting solicitor J.Bosson pointed out that others who had been splashed by the liquid had had to go to a local doctor for treatment. Bosson reckoned the attacks to be 'a low, cowardly act of blackguardism.' He went on to explain that the liquid was 'sulphate of carbon' which smelt 'of double distilled onion juice' - it 'stank enough to clear a crowd and he dared say this was Neill's object.' The case then took an unexpected path when Pidgeon announced that the police had pressured him into bringing the case and he was withdrawing from it immediately!

Neill, however, had to stay in court as other complainants including a Mrs.Lethaby and Sydney Burnell then appeared and accused him of throwing a 'burning liquid' into their faces. The defending solicitor J.Brewer explained how his client had purchased the liquid to repair some punctures in his bicycle tyres and had forgotten all about it until he was at the religious meeting and noticed a strong smell of 'rotten eggs'. He then realised the cork had come loose from the bottle and so he took it from his pocket and 'merely kept it in his hand whilst listening to the speeches.' He denied absolutely throwing it at people.

This version of events was supported by George Moore a blacksmith who had been standing next to Neill and 'was quite sure he saw nothing.' Another member of the crowd William Mingo also denied that Neill had thrown any liquid about as did John Babb. The last witness was Frederick Tucker who had seen Pidgeon come up to Neill and say 'If I know it was you who threw that stuff over me I should knock you in the eye' - which if nothing else seemed to show that there was some sort of question as to whether Neill had been to blame.

The chief magistrate then summed up saying that the evangelical meeting was illegal - but that 'did not justify private individuals such as Neill thoughtlessly going into a crowd and throwing about stuff in a very stupid way.' He therefore found Neill guilty and fined him 7/6 (37.5p) for his alarmingly idiotic actions.

LAW AND ORDER

59. An Inspector calls on South Molton

The Victorians were great reformers. Nothing seems to have escaped their zeal for reformation - indeed improvement was a key principle in their whole social system. This extended even to prisons, there being a Government Inspector of Prisons. In 1851 this official reported on his visits to Bideford, Barnstaple and South Molton to view the places of detention in each. In South Molton the first place he visited was the Borough Gaol and House of Correction in East Street which had been built in 1828-9 at the then huge cost of £2000. His report began by noting that the prison was too small to allow 'the classification of prisoners required by the law' - a reference to the system of grading inmates and providing suitable conditions for each.

On the ground floor there were 4 cells for men that opened out into two small 'airing yards' where the prisoners could exercise. Above these were 4 'rooms' for women but they had no exercise area. The male cells were floored with lime-ash and each held an iron bedstead and bedding. Only one contained a fire-place, the rest being 'destitute of all means of artificial warmth or ventilation.' The cell with the grate also contained a bell to summon the gaoler - the others had none. The female accommodation consisted of 3 cells and a small 'day room' though again only one room contained a fireplace and bell.

In the yards there were two 'very damp and cold' semi-derelict sheds where the men crushed bones for use in agriculture. It was reckoned that each prisoner could crush 28 lbs a day and the revenue from sales of this bone ash amounted to £5 per year. The only prisoner present at the time of the Inspector's visit, a sheep-stealer serving 9 months, was 'suffering from a severe attack of catarrh' brought on by his bone-crushing work. This man would have been receiving the allotted weekly allowance of food viz. 124 ozs of bread, 28 ozs of milk, 1 lb of bacon and 7 lbs of potatoes. Women and children under 12 (!) received the same all bar 14 ozs of bread. Vagrants of both sexes got just 1¾ lbs of bread and ¾ pint of milk and water a day.

No chaplain or schoolmaster attended the prisoners so they were 'entirely destitute of moral and religious instruction' though a surgeon came to check their health 3 times a week. The town magistrates inspected the prison at least once a month and the gaoler received wages of £40 per year.

Because of all the faults identified the Inspector urged the immediate closure of the prison with all future prisoners being sent to Exeter. As he pointed out this wouldn't be too expensive as over the two previous years the prison had only held 6 men and 2 women, plus some short-tern inmates.

The Inspector also visited the 'Lock-up house' which was evidently part of the police station which itself was next to the prison. There were only two cells which bizarrely were 'built of wood lined with sheet iron.' Not surprisingly they were 'exceedingly cold and damp' and the Inspector reckoned anyone confined in them would soon suffer ill-health. Additionally anyone standing in the bakery next door could easily chat to the prisoners. Over the previous two years some 55 men and 10 women had passed through these cells - usually, if the columns of the *Journal* are to be believed, for being drunk and disorderly in the streets of South Molton. The Inspector again recommended that usage of these cells should be discontinued suggesting that the Borough Gaol could be adapted to provide new police cells.

Action did follow and the iron-lined cells were abandoned with all short-term prisoners being held in the refurbished Borough Gaol premises. This was clear evidence clearly of the reforming zeal of our Victorian ancestors - and doubtless a welcome series of changes to the less law-abiding South Moltonians of the past

North Devon Journal 18.5.2000.

60. Baby killing in Barnstaple

The killing of a baby by its mother has always been viewed with horror - yet in earlier centuries the crime was not uncommon especially where young unmarried mothers had to face the condemnation of society for becoming pregnant. Infanticide must have seemed an easy if illegal way out of their shame. Cases in North Devon were just as common as in the rest of Britain.

On June 27th 1853, for example, 12 year old Philip Dyer of Newport was fishing in the River Taw when he hooked a large canvas bag tied up with string. Hauling it ashore and opening it he was horrified to find the body of a female baby inside, along with a large stone which had been weighing it down. He immediately ran home to fetch help and came across Richard Eames and his brother.

At first the two young men refused to believe the boy saying 'It must be somebody's cat'. Philip's insistence, however, finally caused them to go and see for themselves and they realised his story was true. Picking up the bag they carried it to Thomas Torr, a local surgeon, who had it taken to the police station. Here closer examination revealed some strips of printed cloth along with the body and stone.

Superintendent Byron Aldham, head of the Barnstaple police, immediately made inquiries around the town and 'in consequence of information received' went with P.c.Chanter at 1 o'clock in the morning, to arrest 23-year old Eliza Jones. On searching her room the two policemen found a printed cloth dress whose design matched that on the cloth found with the dead baby. Eliza, who was the daughter of a Barnstaple cabinetmaker, was taken off to the borough gaol.

Here she was examined by Dr. Torr who rapidly came to the conclusion that she had given birth to a child within the last fortnight. His conclusion was supported by the prison surgeon Michael Cooke who also examined her.

Three days later the inquest was held and here Dr. Torr, who had carried out a post-mortem on the corpse, related his findings. The baby was new-born, weighed 7 lbs and had certainly breathed and thus had been born alive. There were no actual wounds but blood had gathered under the skin on the skull which suggested some violent injury to the head. He at first reckoned this to be the cause of death but persistent questioning by Eliza's lawyer caused him to become less dogmatic in his view.

Also at the inquest various witnesses came forward to tell what they knew. Thus Sarah French, who was the wife of a baker and who lived in the same house as Eliza, recounted how three months previously she had noticed the girl looking 'much stouter than usual'. Other people also noticed and the general opinion was that 'she had the appearance of a person in the family way.' At the end of June when Sarah saw Eliza out in the backyard of the house 'there was much difference in her shape'. In fact 'she was looking much thinner and more delicate than usual'. Her evidence was corroborated by Ann Hodsoll, the wife of a Barnstaple watchmaker, who was in no doubt from her own observations, that Eliza was pregnant and had subsequently given birth to a child. The inquest jury didn't take long to return their verdict of 'wilful murder'.

Following this Eliza appeared before the magistrates who, surprisingly, committed her for trial at the County Assizes in Exeter on the lesser charge of 'concealment of birth' - possibly on compassionate grounds but more likely owing to the doubts expressed by Dr.Torr. At the Assizes in late July Eliza was brought up and, even though all the evidence seemed to be totally clear, was acquitted by the jury on the basis that this evidence was inadequate to find her guilty.

Birth outside of marriage is extremely common today, yet the crime of infanticide has become very rare - surely a sign that we live in a more civilized and compassionate society.
North Devon Journal 18.1.2001

61. Two young horse thieves

One of the commoner crimes today is car stealing - generally carried out by young people seeking a cheap thrill or showing off to their friends. It might be thought that this sort of crime only began with the growth in car ownership - yet even when our society was based around horses such crimes occurred. In August 1854 a brother and sister, Azariah and Catherine Williams, were arrested and charged with horse-stealing at Berrynarbor. The boy was just 13 and the girl 10 and the story that came out showed that this theft was not just thrill seeking.

At the committal hearing the two were said to be vagrants 'without father, mother or anybody to take care of them' who survived by 'singing, begging, and thieving for bread.' These unfortunate children had been in Berrynarbor one lunchtime when Henry Squire, who worked for a Mr Hancock, was having his meal and had left some horses to graze. The two took the opportunity to steal a black mare and with his sister perched on its back the boy led it off towards Combe Martin. When Squire returned he told his master of his loss and Hancock rushed off to follow the thieves.

He caught them up near Trentishoe and asked Azariah whose horse it was - to which the boy brazenly answered 'Mine'. When challenged, however, he ran off crying out 'Mamma' but Hancock soon caught him and brought both him and his sister before the local magistrates.

Here they recounted their story. Their father had been a miner in Merthyr Tydfil but had died and their mother took them to Exeter where 'she left them entirely to themselves, and went away with a soldier'. Forced to become beggars they had ended up in North Devon, where they took the horse. The magistrates were rather at a loss to know what to do with them, never having had such young horse thieves appear in court, but they eventually committed them for trial at the next Quarter Sessions.

This came off a month later when Azariah and Catherine, now described as 'two extremely diminutive children', appeared in the courtroom in Barnstaple Guildhall where their heads 'scarcely reached the low partition which separates the prisoners from the jury'. They seemed oblivious of the gravity of their situation as they 'inattentively looked about and frequently smiled at each other and the persons who surrounded them' - in fact they just appeared to be acting their age.

Mr Hancock, as the prosecution witness, told the story of how he missed his horse and caught the thieves and the children did not contradict any of the details. The *Journal* report doesn't indicate that they were even asked for their version of events which seems extremely odd.

The jury immediately returned a guilty verdict and the chairman of the bench made his summing up saying 'this was one of the most painful cases which had ever come before the Court'. Painful though it was, it didn't stop him announcing that 'There was nothing now left but that a severe sentence should be passed.'

Apparently because they had been 'bereft of that tender care which a mother ought to have afforded them' it was now the duty of the court 'to throw around them that care and protection which had been neglected by their natural protector.' This, unbelievably, took the form of 'Four years penal servitude' in Exeter Prison!

Modern readers will probably be left open-mouthed at this sentence, bearing in mind the two children's ages and their unfortunate life histories. The 'good old days' are definitely old - but good? I leave that to you to decide.
North Devon Journal 22.2.2001

62. The mad murderer of Northam

In August 1855 the *Journal* carried the chilling headline 'DREADFUL MURDER'. Philippa Hancock of Northam had been found in her one-bedroomed hovel with her head beaten in with a hammer and her throat cut. The report goes on to say, 'There was no second thought as to whose hand had perpetrated the bloody deed' as a search was instantly mounted for her husband Robert.

After murdering his wife he had fled stopping only to tell his brother-in-law Philip Dennis what he had done. The only thing he carried from the house was his razor - in order to commit suicide. His nerve failed, however, and he hid in a barn at Knapp near the River Torridge.

On the alarm being raised the entire parish turned out to search for him they being marshalled by Superintendant Tyrell of the Bideford police force who had been called in to help, there being no resident policeman in the village at this date. The fugitive was eventually discovered by a man called Parkhouse and arrested by the parish constable Braund. He offered no resistance and his fellow villagers did not try to attack him. The shock that passed through the village following the news was profound - 'the oldest inhabitant never recollected a murder in Northam, there was not even the tradition of such an awful crime having been committed there.'

At the coroner's inquest and later at his trial a pathetic story emerged. Robert was a 46 year old labourer who worked as a 'heaver' unloading boats at Appledore and Bideford. Following his marriage to Philippa some 20 years earlier they had had two children both of whom were 'in service' elsewhere at the time of the murder. The couple's poverty was extreme as their 'cottage' merely consisted of a kitchen downstairs and a bedroom above.

During the two years leading up to the crime Robert and Philippa had 'led a miserable life' constantly quarrelling, with the husband 'breathing out against her threatening and slaughter' under the impression that 'she was too familiar with a man who once lived a near neighbour to them.' Robert's jealousy had been inflamed by his workmates who apparently kept teasing him about his wife's supposed infidelities. On some days the distraught man had actually run home two or three times believing that his rival had secretly turned up to see his wife. Indeed their relationship had become so tense that several months before the couple had separated - but then got back together again.

At the inquest it was noted that Philippa had been a very strong woman who had recently been working at unloading stones from ships - 'an employment morally and physically debasing to females.' As such it was thought that Robert must have attacked her as she slept otherwise she could have fought him off.

After his arrest he was removed to Exeter to await trial at the County Assizes. At his departure from Northam his two children had wished him a tearful farewell whilst the whole village stood looking on in silence - 'the general feeling being one of pity for him and his wife - that they should be the victims of their own folly and the gibes of others.'

On his way to Exeter 'his heart broke down completely, his resignation to his fate forsook him, the terrors of death got hold of him, and the dread of the gallows was, he said, more than he could bear.' The law, however, was inexorable and he had to stand trial in December knowing that the hangman awaited.

His lawyers entered a plea of insanity and the evidence was gone though in great detail especially the material about Robert's insane rages where he had pulled his hair out by the roots and destroyed his own rather pitiful belongings. Dr.Bucknill of the County Lunatic Asylum reported on his examination of Robert saying that it was clear the man suffered 'delusions' and was in the grip of some 'religious' frenzy as he rambled on about meeting his wife's 'lover' on the Day of Judgement. His professional view was that Robert 'seems to be under hallucination, to see and hear things which have no existence in fact.'

Following this evidence the judge spent over 2 hours summing up the case in great detail stressing that by their verdict the jury would either consign Robert 'to the mad-house for the remainder of his days' or 'would send him to the gallows.' The jury retired for an hour and then filed back into the court where their foreman, when asked the question 'How say you gentlemen, is Robert Hancock guilty or not guilty?' replied 'Guilty of Murder'. An 'awful pause intervened' before the foreman added 'we find he committed it whilst under an illusion.'

The judge thanked them and then sentenced Robert as an insane criminal 'to be detained during her Majesty's pleasure'. How long the unfortunate man lived I do not know but that he had to live with his actions for the rest of his life is clear - and that this knowledge must have been terrible indeed.
North Devon Journal 4.11.1999

63. Dirty deeds at Combe Martin

'The Donkey Poisoning Case at Combe Martin' isn't one of the lost cases of Sherlock Holmes but a true event that occurred in July 1856. Robert Hole, described as 'an elderly man, of mild and somewhat respectable appearance', was alleged to have given 'corrosive sublimate' (a mercury based chemical) to a donkey owned by James Jewell. He was tried at the Devon Assizes in September following his arrest when the following facts were recounted.

In 1855 a civil court case had been heard to decide the tenancy of a meadow known as Floodgate in Combe Martin. At this it was decided that Robert Hole, the parish churchwarden, was the legal tenant of three-quarters with the Reverend John Pyke, rector of Parracombe, having claim to the remainder. Hole had tried to rent the other quarter but there had been a disagreement about the rent and so the clergyman used it to graze his own cattle and other beasts belonging to the local people. Hole evidently let his feelings fester.

All this was related by the Reverend Pyke who was then followed by William Creek a farmer who also kept an inn in Combe Martin. Following the original court case he grazed his brother's horse in that part of the meadow leased by the Reverend Pyke but it had to be destroyed after its leg was broken. Creek 'thought the injury had not been produced by the kick from a horse' as was suggested at the time.

Soon after a donkey grazing the same land died - 'its head was swollen and its tongue protruded from its mouth.' A sheep then died, then a pig and then Jewell's donkey and another horse. He noted that none of Hole's animals being grazed on the rest of the meadow had died.

The donkey's tongue, windpipe and part of its lungs were removed, 'put into a butter-pot' and taken by Creek to a Mr.Herapath, an analytical chemist in Bristol. Creek also deposed that Ann Dendle had told him that she had seen 'Farmer Hole' drive the donkey into a barn on the meadow just before it was taken ill.

Ann herself then appeared and recounted how she had been returning home about 10 p.m. on 3rd July when Hole rode past her. For some reason she turned and followed him taking care to remove her white bonnet so she wouldn't be noticed. It was then that she saw Hole take the donkey into the barn although what he then did she couldn't say. She did, however, add that it was said in the village that 'God Almighty had given up Farmer Hole to the devil for seven years.'

Evidence then came from a variety of local people that Hole had warned them to remove their animals from Floodgate

Meadow as 'accidents happened there' - a veiled threat that came back to haunt him.

Two Barnstaple policemen then gave their account of how they had gone to Hole's farm and removed a variety of suspicious looking items including a ball of grease and slices of mouldy bread stuck together with some substance. They were followed by William Herapath the chemist who had analysed the donkey's remains and found mercury in the tongue. No animals would naturally eat the substance and it was present in such quantity that it must have been deliberately administered to the poor animal. He had also analysed the items discovered by the police and found them to contain mercury.

Faced with all this the defence pointed out that there was no evidence to prove Hole had poisoned the animals. Ann Dendle's evidence as to seeing Hole and the donkey together was false and had been concocted merely to gain a reward. His neighbours all disliked Hole and had taken this opportunity to have their revenge. The police had waited 26 days before arresting Hole and it was well-known that all farmers used mercury to treat their sheep for scab. Conviction on such scanty 'evidence' would be unfair and would 'destroy his nearest and dearest interests, destroy his hitherto irreproachable character and consign him from the church-wardenship and the position he held in his parish to the lowest possible pitch of degradation.'

Fine words but following a full summing-up the jury only took a few minutes to find Hole guilty as charged and the judge imposed a sentence of 'Penal Servitude for four years' which was increased to six the next day after the judge had checked the Act of Parliament dealing with this crime! Harsh perhaps but only a year or so previously Hole would have been transported for between 10 and 15 years.

Thus the churchwarden came to his ignoble end - clearly he wasn't likeable but one hopes the circumstantial evidence would be backed by better forensic evidence today.

North Devon Journal 8.4.1999

64. Suicide after attempted murder at Eastdown

The human mind and its workings is still a great mystery to us. Throughout history irrational behaviour has often led to tragedy, a case in point occurring in the parish of Eastdown near Arlington in October 1857.

In that month Henry Featherstone a farm labourer who worked for Richard Passmore of Wigmore Farm attempted to murder two of his fellow workers and then committed suicide by hanging. As the contemporary report put it, 'No such fearful combination of crime had ever before in the memory of the oldest inhabitant startled or disgraced the neighbourhood.'

As the law demanded an inquest was held under the local coroner Richard Bremridge who heard the various witnesses recount a strange, sad story. The proceedings began with the jury viewing Featherstone's body which the police had taken to the nearest house and left overnight in the corner of the kitchen. The Manning family who lived there apparently had to cook and eat their meals in the same room 'to the terror of the children and the disgust of their parents' - which seems a monumental understatement! The coroner severely criticised the police for their crassness saying that any bodies should be kept in the church house.

After this initial hiccup Richard Passmore appeared as the first witness. He had employed Featherstone for five and a half years without any problem regarding him as a 'quiet and inoffensive person'. A few weeks previously, however, the labourer had begun to complain about what he regarded as unfair treatment by two of Passmore's female servants. On the 22nd of October he suddenly refused to carry out his work and demanded his wages. When asked why he complained that he had been refused anything to eat the night before and that he wasn't going to put up with such actions.

Passmore threatened to take him to court for breaking his work contract but Featherstone merely replied, 'They can only put me to Bridewell [prison] for a month, that's all they or you can do to me, and I shall be clear of all of you; then it will be my turn to have a game with you.' With this cryptic statement he left.

On October 28th two servants were sitting in the kitchen of Passmore's farmhouse when someone fired a gun through the window and then ran off. Luckily, no-one was hit and rushing outside they found a velvet jacket which was identified as belonging to Featherstone. The next day they found a pistol which was 'a heavily constructed weapon' over a foot long. That afternoon Mr.William Tamlyn found the dead man's body swinging from a tree in Knowle Wood.

John Williams, a shoemaker of Berrydown Cross, and his wife then gave their evidence. Featherstone had lodged with them after leaving his master's employ and neither could recall any odd behaviour. They added that the rope used in the hanging had been bought in Barnstaple by the dead man a few days previously which suggested a premeditated suicide.

Joseph Huxtable, landlord of the local pub the Smith's Arms, then appeared to say that Featherstone had been drinking in his pub a few days before he committed suicide. Featherstone had complained about his fellow servants to Huxtable and when asked what he was going to do about it answered obliquely that 'he had something else in his pocket which would master some of them' - presumably a reference to the pistol.

One of Passmore's other servants William Brooks recalled how Featherstone had been 'much disturbed in mind for the last six weeks.' Indeed all his fellow servants thought the dead man was 'getting mazed'.

After listening to the evidence the jury only took ten minutes to return their verdict that Featherstone committed suicide 'not being sound in mind, memory and understanding.' The coroner added that the body 'would be denied the rites of Christian burial, and would be interred between the hours of nine and twelve o'clock at night.'

No real reason for Featherstone's attempt to murder his fellow servants was ever offered but presumably a smouldering feeling of resentment had developed in his mind and one last incident was enough to push him over the edge into crime and murder but the mystery of his mind's workings just before his death will forever remain just that.

North Devon Journal 20.5.1999

65. A 'wanton, absurd and ridiculous' shooting

The Devon County police force was established in 1856 and for many of its earliest years found it difficult to attract suitable candidates to fill the ranks, with many being dismissed for a variety of reasons. One ex-officer who went on to worse things was Amos Tamlyn. In October 1865 he was brought before the County Magistrates at Barnstaple charged with firing a double barrelled shotgun into both the front and rear of Newton Cross House at Newton Tracey then the home of a Captain Hogg!

At the trial the story came out. On 12th of October Tamlyn had been in the Hunters Inn in the parish then kept by Thomas Clarke. The publican recognised him and knew 'no harm of him'. He was carrying a gun and had his dog with him. After a pint of beer he left at about 7 o'clock though the publican wasn't sure 'how fashion' (accurate) his clock was.

On the road outside William Rodd met Tamlyn and walked with him to Newton Tracey village where the two went in to the Huntshaw Inn, had some beer and separated. A little later he was seen and spoken to by Thomas Hoyle outside of Captain Hogg's house. Five minutes later Hoyle heard two gun shots. Asked if the prisoner was the man he had seen he answered evasively 'He is the height of 'em,' and claimed that it had been too dark to see anyone clearly.

George Miles, a servant to Captain Hogg, gave his evidence of hearing two shots and the next morning finding a hole in the back door as well as shattered windows both front and back - which suggests he was deaf and certainly not very observant. Rather oddly he added that he took careful note of the time he heard the shot - though why isn't explained.

Things moved slowly at this period and it wasn't until two days later that Sergeant Sheriff and P.c.Angel had turned up to examine the scene of the crime. They had been handed two bits of paper torn from the *Crewkerne Journal* bearing gun-powder traces that another servant had found by the front gate. After some detective work they fixed on Tamlyn as the probable culprit.

Two days later again the Sergeant found his suspect at the Ship Inn in Barnstaple and casually said to him, 'Tamlyn I want to speak to you, will you take a walk down the street with me?' As they walked along Sheriff asked questions about Tamlyn's movements on the night of the shooting which only confirmed his suspicions. In the words of the contemporary court report 'By that time we had got as far as the lock up, and I then took him into custody' which suggests the Sergeant was a canny policeman.

After giving this evidence Sheriff then recounted how he had searched Tamlyn's lodgings and found pieces of a *Crewkerne Journal* which exactly fitted the pieces found outside Captain Hogg's house. Sheriff had also extracted the shot from the Captain's walls and doors and this also matched that found in Tamlyn's possession.

The prisoner had been lodging with his uncle Henry Woollacott of Tawstock and he was summoned to give evidence - which didn't help the prosecution case much. Indeed when asked if he recognised the *Crewkerne Journal* as his nephew's he said he didn't adding that he couldn't say 'whether the police brought it there or not themselves.' He also couldn't be sure what time his lodger arrived home on the night in question as 'We were rather short of candle that night, so I could not see the time, and I was obliged to go to bed in the dark.'

The prosecution case didn't really need his evidence, however, and Tamlyn was rapidly found guilty. A last minute plea by his lawyer that the shooting had been 'wanton, absurd and ridiculous' rather than malicious helped reduce his punishment - which was two months with hard labour in the local House of Correction.

As the ex-policeman was taken away the magistrates and Captain Hogg said how satisfied they were with 'the able and zealous manner' of Sheriff and Angel - though why Tamlyn actually fired the shots in the first place was never explained.
North Devon Journal 29.7.1999

66. Devon Police

Compared to many areas of the world Britain is a very law abiding nation where most people both respect the police and assume we always have had a constabulary. In Devon, as with most counties, the police force as we understand it today only dates from 1856. In that year the Devon County force was established though many old boroughs, especially in North Devon, kept their own small forces most of which had been set up 20 years or so before.

Each year the Government-appointed Inspector of Constabulary published his 'Report' and the one for 1869 makes interesting reading. The County personnel totalled 334 men including one Chief Constable on £400 p.a., his Deputy on £156 p.a., 13 Superintendants, 34 Sergeants and 285 Constables - just one of whom was 'generally employed in detective duties.' Every officer below the rank of Superintendant received 5d per week 'to supply themselves with boots.' These were the men who patrolled the North Devon countryside along with Ilfracombe and Holsworthy.

The Inspector also visited all of the borough towns which still ran their own forces and reported on them. Thus in Barnstaple he found a force of ten men run by a Head Constable on £120 a year, a sergeant on 24/- (£1.20) a week and 8 constables on weekly wages varying between 17/- and 18/- (85-90p). The force may have been small but crime had actually fallen over the year and the men were said to be 'in an efficient state.'

Bideford on the other hand employed just two policemen - a Head Constable on £72.16.0 (£72.80) a year and one constable on 18/- a week. Amazingly to us, perhaps, that only one criminal ended up in court that week with just 23 other people being proceeded against for various misdemeanours. The town had 52 public houses (hence the name the 'Pack of Cards' known to many older Bidefordians) which were 'well conducted'. Unfortunately whilst the town council had drawn up plans to build a new police station to replace the old one in the Town Hall nothing had happened and the Inspector noted 'The present cells are quite unsuitable for the detention of prisoners.' This, however, wasn't as bad as his observation that 'The police force is quite inadequate in number to provide for the proper watching and protection of the borough.'

If this was bad, Torrington was even worse. Like Bideford the town had a two man police force one of whom earned £1 a week and the other 16/- (80p). The Inspector bluntly stated 'There is no efficiently organised police force in this borough.' This comment possibly stemmed from the surprising fact that the Inspector wasn't provided with any figures about crime in the borough at all as they do not appear to have been kept! He finished his damning summary by writing 'This borough, in order to ensure any degree of police efficiency should, for police purposes, be placed under the charge of the constabulary of the county.' Ouch!

South Molton was better but not by much. The town was another with a two man force with the Head Constable earning £78 a year and his constable on 16/6 (82.5p) a week. Apparently 'The officers of this force are extremely respectable' which seems an odd comment and makes one wonder what, for example, the police in Barnstaple were like. Additionally the men were 'very desirous to perform their duty satisfactorily' but the Inspector reckoned that just two men couldn't hope to properly patrol the borough.

Over the rest of the century three of the boroughs joined the Devon County force; Torrington in 1870 (and again in 1886 but that's another story!), South Molton in 1877 and Bideford in 1889. Barnstaple didn't finally join until 1921 but by then the idea that we didn't have a police force would have been unimaginable.

67. Jack the Ripper and Barnstaple

In June 1892 readers of the *North Devon Journal* were doubtless horrified to read an article headed, 'Attempt to blackmail Dr. Harper'. The doctor in question lived in Bear Street in Barnstaple, being one of the town's leading citizens and almost certainly its most eminent medical man.

The blackmailer was a Dr. Thomas Neill Cream who had written a letter to Joseph Harper concerning his son W.H. Harper who was then just completing his studies as a medical student in London and who was a lodger in the same house as Cream. Two young prostitutes had been poisoned with strychnine a few days earlier near Waterloo and Cream wrote to claim he had evidence of the involvement of Harper junior. He wrote bluntly, 'I am willing to give you the said evidence, so that you can suppress it, for £1500 sterling.' The letter was signed 'W.H. Murray' and said Harper senior would be contacted again if he placed an advertisement in the *Daily Chronicle* reading 'W.H.M. Will pay you for your services - Dr. H.'

Joseph Harper, however, after consulting his solicitor, went straight to the police but in those days forensic science was in its infancy and little progress could be made in tracing the writer. The threatening letter, once it became known, caused the *Journal*'s editor to write, 'The attempt to blackmail Dr. Harper, who is esteemed and respected throughout North Devon, has given rise to general expressions of indignation.'

A few days after writing this first letter Cream wrote to the coroner handling the inquest on the two dead girls again claiming that Harper junior was their murderer. He again signed the letter as 'W.H. Murray'. By this time, however, and for various reasons unconnected to Harper detectives were becoming interested in Cream and began following him. He actually got his solicitor to send a protest to Scotland Yard but the police continued to shadow him.

On June 1 the London detectives travelled to Braunton where the younger Dr. Harper had just begun practising and, following an interview with him, put all their clues together and realised that Cream not only wrote the blackmail/accusatory letters but was also probably the real murderer. Not having enough evidence for a murder trial they got Harper to agree to act as a witness against his former fellow-lodger on a charge of blackmail. This allowed them to arrest Cream only days before he was due to sail to America and freedom.

On June 4 Cream was charged with blackmail but the case was adjourned until another dead prostitute linked to Cream had been exhumed and strychnine found in her body. This led to Cream being charged with murder - a charge that came to trial at the Old Bailey four months later. Cream was found guilty partly on the basis of the blackmail letter sent to Barnstaple and was hanged a few days later.

The two Dr. Harpers continued practising in North Devon for many years afterwards and that would have been the end of the story but for one very mysterious and hotly debated occurrence. On the gallows just before the trapdoor opened the hangman is said to have heard Cream claim to be Jack the Ripper - which conjures up the appalling thought that if Harper had been suspected of Cream's murders he might also have been accused of the fearful Ripper murders - 'Barnstaple Jack' is a chilling thought.

North Devon Journal 17.12.1998

68. The gipsy shooting in Barnstaple

North Devon is a generally peaceful place - indeed its air of tranquillity attracts many here both on holidays and to live. Occasionally, however, there is an episode as violent as any seen in our large cities. One such occurred in Barnstaple in July 1933 when Frederick Pow killed John Small and went on trial for his life at Exeter the following November.

Small was one of a family of gipsies who lived in a camp at Cudmore's Field near where Forches estate now stands in Barnstaple. Some time before the main events in this story Mr.Newcombe, landlord of the Mermaid Hotel, had lent £1 to Albert Moss who also lived at the camp. Pow was the landlord's friend and offered to get the money back.

He soon located Moss who agreed to repay the loan but promptly disappeared. At 8 p.m. the same day Pow and Newcombe went to the Union Inn, near the Derby lace factory which was a well-known gipsy haunt, to find him. Moss did in fact turn up but Reuben Small, brother of John, warned him that Pow and Newcombe were looking for him and he didn't enter the pub.

When Pow heard what Reuben had done he said 'We will go around to the Mermaid. We will get half a dozen men and break up the camp.' Half an hour later he was seen outside the Union Inn saying, 'I am going up to the camp to have his blood.' On saying this he produced 'a most extraordinary gun' from under his coat. It was an old-fashioned rifle with its barrel shortened and its stock lengthened. The gipsies in the pub hurried after him as he went towards their camp and one, John Small, came up close to Pow who fired at him and then clubbed him as he lay on the ground. Small died of his wounds five days later. After the shot was fired a crowd of men rushed Pow and disarmed him but he then escaped and wasn't recaptured until 2 days later.

At his trial he denied murder and various witnesses recounted the events as they had seen them. Moses Small, another of the dead man's brothers, alleged that Pow had threatened 'Stand back or I will kill the lot of you' before he deliberately fired at John. A dummy dressed in John's bloodstained clothes was then produced in court to show the dead man's wounds - at which Moses broke down in tears.

John Scoines of Newington Street who was a friend of Pow said he had tried to take the gun away but Pow had shouted 'Stand back or I will blow your guts out'. It was just after this that Small was shot. Albert Offield of Prince's Street said he saw John Small hit Pow on the face before Pow pulled out his gun whilst Sarah Casinelli recounted how Small had tried to wrestle the gun from Pow before it went off.

In his own defence Pow said that on the day of the shooting he had been 'on the drink' from 11 a.m. to 9 p.m. adding that he had only taken the gun with him to frighten off the gipsies after Reuben Small had told him that if he went to the camp 'We will ____ well kill you.' He claimed that he was actually trying to remove the cartridge from the gun when Small rushed him and the gun went off in the scuffle that followed. He had run away afterwards as the gun 'was not licensed' and he was afraid of the consequences.

His lawyer then posed the rhetorical question 'What would happen with the jury if they were threatened and advanced upon by a crowd of strong, active young fellows who were furiously angry?' which rather ignored the fact that Frederick had brought about the situation himself. They, the jury, had heard very conflicting evidence and as 'there was so much confusion' they should not find his client guilty of murder.

After just 25 minutes the jury found Pow not guilty on the capital charge but guilty of manslaughter. The judge then said to Pow 'You have been very close to the peril of the verdict of murder and sentence of death.' As it was he had killed another man whilst under the influence of drink and as such he had to be severely punished. With this he sentenced Pow to eight years penal servitude reckoning that the sentence was 'a lenient one'. So ended one the rare trials for murder in North Devon.

North Devon Journal 4.5.2000

69. The Coroner

Coroners are one of the oldest legal officers in Britain. Oddly, however, their records were always viewed as their own private property and because of this few collections of inquest papers have been preserved in our record offices. If you have an interest in such cases the best source is probably the newspaper and the *Journal* made a point of covering all local inquests - many of which reveal pathetic stories of loss and sadness.

One, held in Braunton Parish Room in June 1899 regarding the death of a Mrs.Rottenbury combined elements of both. Only four witnesses appeared but their evidence paints a complete story of a disappointed woman. The coroner in this case was Dr.E.Slade-King and his first witness was John Rottenbury a gardener of Ilfracombe who identified the dead woman as his 55 year old wife. He had last seen her alive at 1.30 p.m. nine days before when she had left their home with the parting words 'she was going out to Hillsborough to drown herself'. John's callous answer had been 'I hope you'll do it.' As if this wasn't bad enough he went on to admit that they had rowed about money and 'he had threatened to murder her.'

This threat had been uttered because John was illiterate and during their 14 years of marriage his wife had 'outwitted' him over money. They had taken lodgers for 7 years who had brought in some £20 per year which he had thought was being banked. Imagine his anger when he found it had all gone - and he himself was deemed responsible for some £30 of debt his wife had managed to run up. He had been cruelly deceived even though he 'had been so good as a king to her' or so he claimed. Unfortunately in the last two years she had 'given way to drink' and had on many previous occasions threatened to 'make away with herself.'

Their marriage was obviously a second one for her as the next inquest witness was Ernest Tucker an Ilfracombe coach painter and son of the deceased. He immediately contradicted his stepfather saying he had never heard his mother threaten to commit suicide. He then read out a letter he had received the morning after his mother's body was found. It simply said 'Dear Ernest and Ann, I dare not face Jack's anger, so I shall take poison tonight. I shall be found in a field between Barnstaple and Braunton where I can get out of anyone seeing me. Do not think too hard of what you hear. I shall try to get as near Braunton as I can. I feel too broken-hearted to live, for he swore he would murder me tonight. I feel sure he will. From your broken-hearted mother.' Jack was evidently the name she used for her husband. Ernest added that he knew of no reason for her to be 'broken hearted' and that she was not 'in the habit of drinking.'

The next witness was James Reed a Wrafton farmer who was at work when some children came to tell him there was a 'tramp' in the field near his house. He went to see who this was and found a woman's dead body along with two bottles. One of the bottles was labelled 'Carbolic Acid' and was empty whilst the other contained gin. Reed immediately fetched Police Sergeant Jeffery from Braunton.

Jeffery then took the witness stand. He described how the body first appeared - with poison 'oozing out of the mouth'. In the pocket of her dress he found a note and a purse. The note simply stated 'This is to let anyone know I am Mrs.Rottenbury of 2, Foxbeare, Ilfracombe, going to die because I am broken-hearted.' He later made inquiries and found she had left Ilfracombe for Braunton on the train the day before carrying some carbolic acid she had purchased in her home town telling the shopkeeper 'she wanted it for disinfecting purposes.'

After hearing all this evidence the coroner summed up the case reckoning it 'was one of the most carefully planned and deliberate suicides he had ever known.' The jury, under a Captain

Gould Clarke, quickly returned their verdict of suicide and so poor Mrs.Rottenbury (nowhere is her Christian name given) disappears into history, her memory only kept alive by a short report in the *Journal*'s columns - how transient is human life!

70. A double tragedy at the Exeter Inn

In February 1912 *Journal* readers were doubtless shocked to read the headline 'Terrible Double Tragedy at Barnstaple' which concerned a murder and suicide at the Exeter Inn in Litchdon Street in the town.

At 5.30 p.m. one Wednesday evening people living in the street heard two gunshots a minute apart and then saw Mrs.Worth the publican's wife running across the street to the tailor's shop kept by Ernest Dyer. He hurried into the pub's bar and found Frederick Blake lying dead with a shotgun wound to his head; making his way through to the garage at the back of the premises he then found the landlord George Worth with the top of his head blown off and a double barrelled shotgun lying nearby.

At the inquest a tragic story came out. Blake, a 33 year old labourer who lived nearby at Barbican Place, had been doing casual work at the Exeter Inn on market days as well as being a regular customer. His labour was needed because, as Blake's widow put it, her husband's employer was often 'indisposed' which was a polite euphemism for being drunk. Asked about the relationship between her husband and Worth Mrs.Blake had to admit that they had often 'come to blows' and Worth had threatened to shoot Blake. This was usually after Blake had stepped in to prevent Worth 'behaving violently' to his wife.

Following the widow's evidence a drayman who had delivered beer to the pub only 45 minutes before the murder gave his evidence. Worth had been totally sober and signed as normal for the delivery. He had seen no gun whilst in the building.

Mrs.Worth then gave her account. Asked directly by the coroner whether her husband had been 'somewhat violent' when drunk she admitted that was so although she knew of no 'bad feeling' between him and Blake. She also denied ever having heard her husband threaten to shoot Blake.

She then recounted how her husband hadn't got up until 1 p.m. on the fatal day and how he had brought his 'ordinary sporting cock barrel gun' into the bar about 5 p.m. Asked why he did this she replied, 'He had some fresh cartridges, and was going to see how they answered. I didn't take very much notice of it.' A member of the coroner's jury helpfully suggested that Worth had been 'trying the size of the cartridges'.

She hadn't actually seen the fatal shot and indeed thought Blake had merely fainted following it. It was only when she went over to help him up that she realised he had been injured. Worth said nothing after the shot went off - about which a jury member commented 'It seems funny, shooting a man and not saying anything.' Her last piece of evidence was a denial that Blake had stepped in to protect her from her alcoholic husband - which seems to have been a rather pathetic attempt to protect a sick man's tarnished reputation.

The police then gave their evidence about the appearance of the bodies in the bar and shed. Worth had apparently been lying down when he committed suicide 'because blood and brains were blown out of the door and into the adjoining shed.'

The coroner's summing up was carefully phrased - Worth 'unfortunately drank a great deal too much at times', although he appeared sober 'he was not very well', it was 'a remarkable thing' to think Blake had been accidentally shot and so on. The jury only took a few minutes to find that Blake had been 'wilfully murdered' by Worth who had then 'whilst temporarily insane' committed suicide.

The burial of the two men took place several days later at the Holy Trinity churchyard where they were interred only a few yards apart. A huge crowd turned out but only the direct mourners were allowed in to the graveyard. Here both burial services were read by the Reverend Every - and so ended one of the most terrible tragedies to hit Barnstaple before the First World War.
North Devon Journal 29.10.1998

ODDS AND ENDS

71. Settlement examinations at Parkham

Today we think it nothing unusual to move to some far distant place in Britain in search of a new job or whatever - and never think about asking permission of the State to do so. In the past, however, if you were poor (and most were) you couldn't legally move without first obtaining a settlement certificate. This was a legal document where your home parish agreed to take you back and provide care if through illness or age you couldn't support yourself.

Every parish generally has a selection of these documents amongst its records and Parkham is no exception. Thus in 1672 Phillipa Tovey of Northam was 'desirous to goe & Lyve with her brother in law Thomas Rogers' in Parkham. Northam agreed to accept her back if she 'doe happen to become chargeable & need releife.' Six years later William Tardrew of Buckland Brewer a miller was 'disirous to remove for some tyme with his wife and Children, and to reside within the parish of parkham. . . where he hopes to get a better livelihood.' In order to get these certificates people had to appear before a local magistrate and recite their life history in order that the legal place of settlement could be decided. Copies were given to the people involved and these too have ended up in parish chests.

Typical is that for John Jolliffe, a pauper of Parkham, recorded in 1797. Born in East Putford he was apprenticed aged just 7 to John Stapledon of Buckland Brewer. His master died about 11 years later and John was hired by Thomas Fry at the princely wages of £3.3.0 per year He then worked for Henry Cleverdon for £4.4.0 a year and later went to work for William Braund. He then married Christian Lee and saw his wages rise to 1/- a day, presumably as his skills improved. These constant moves from one job to another were very common amongst our ancestors and help dispel the myth that people never moved - even if their movements were very localised.

One of these settlement examinations as they are known is fascinating in the details it gives us about one person. In May 1819

Jasper Pickard recorded his history. Born in Parkham he was apprenticed aged 8 or 9 to Thomas Cann. Soon after he moved to Shebbear - where William Becklake employed him for two years until he fell ill with fever and returned home. Recovering he was next employed by his uncle Jasper Pridham of East Putford at £3 per year. In 1805 he took up a job in Northam with William Partridge - a job he followed with a succession of similar posts until he apprenticed himself as a mariner to Samuel Vernon, master of the *Concord* of Barnstaple. For some reason this only lasted 3 months before he 'ran away' from his master and got a job with Lawrence Pridham, presumably another relative, in Chulmleigh.

A few further short term jobs in that area followed and he then moved to Bridgwater to work with Thomas Gulliver. After only seven weeks, however, Jasper had an unspecified 'accident' and returned home to Parkham. Over his accident he returned to Chulmleigh where various employers hired him on the understanding that he was 'allowed to return to Parkham during the Season for Herring Fishing' (then an important local industry) - a seasonal pattern of movement he followed for quite a few years before going to a magistrate to record his life story.

A second document amongst the Parkham material records that some time over these years Jasper had managed to marry Ann and have five children within eleven years. Here then is one poor man's complete life history. It is interesting to reflect that even though our ancestors may well have been very poor they still have left such plentiful records in the form of these settlement documents.

North Devon Journal 18.12.1999

72. Work for the gravedigger in Ilfracombe

Edward Clogg, the gravedigger of Ilfracombe had his work cut out to keep up with the demands for his services in July 1741. The reason was simple - smallpox. It is the first disease we have ever completely cleansed from the world but 250 years ago it was a killer.

The parish register for Ilfracombe shows burials running at an average of 40 per year from 1737 to 1740. In 1741, however, the total jumps to 104. The register shows the first death from 'Varicolae', as the local vicar termed the disease, occurring in May of that year. The victim was a Sarah Rice she being followed five weeks later by Hannah Challacombe.

Over the six months from June to December 66 deaths from smallpox are recorded along with a further 11 that seem to be due to the same disease. There are no smallpox deaths from December 1741 to May 1742 when the outbreak flared up again and another 8 people succumbed over five months. Certain families seem to have suffered more than others such as the Courtneys who lost 3 including 2 on one day. The Somers, Thomas, Saunders, Stanbury, Andrews and Lake families all had at least 2 fatalities.

Such epidemics were not uncommon in the eighteenth century. Indeed until Edward Jenner introduced vaccination in 1798 the only safeguard against the disease was direct inoculation with live smallpox germs which, in many cases, actually killed those being inoculated.

Other serious outbreaks are recorded in the Ilfracombe parish registers for January to July 1751 (44 deaths), June 1760 to January 1761 (34 deaths) and January to May 1768 (25 deaths). No evidence is quoted as to where the outbreaks originated but the disease was endemic and any diseased sailor entering the busy port could have brought the germs with him. There was no effective treatment once you had caught the disease and even if you didn't die you were certainly left scarred for life with hideous gaping depressions in your skin where the pustules had been.

Apart from the parish registers a few other records of these outbreaks have survived. The most intriguing is to be found in the accounts of the Overseers of the Poor for Ilfracombe which are now housed in the North Devon Record Office. In the volume covering 1751 occur a whole series of entries about Mary Harris who was buried on April 24th of that year. She first enters the records on the 1st. of April when she was given 2/- (10p) to help her through 'the Smallpox'. Presumably a pauper she was being offered financial help by the parish officials. Three days later she received another 1/6 (7.5p) and three days afterwards was given another 2/6 (12.5p) being 'in Sickness'. On the 13th she received her last payment of 3/6 (17.5p). Also on that day Jane Hancock, Ann Lewis and Sarah Williams were given various small sums 'for Attending' Mary.

Only two days later Robert Boone was paid 3/9 (19p) 'for 4 1/2 yds of Burying Crape' for Mary's funeral shroud. John Norman was paid 6d (2.5p) 'for bread & Ale at the washing & Laying out' of Mary's body whilst two of her nurses Sarah and Ann were given 1/- each for the actual preparation of the body. The coffin maker William Cross was paid 5/- (25p) and Edward Clogg received 1/- for digging the grave. The final payment was 1/6 for an 'Afidavit'. This was a legal document proving that the corpse had been buried in a woollen shroud. This was necessary as Acts of Parliament in 1666 and 1678 made families liable for a fine if any material other than wool was used - the Act being an attempt to stimulate a declining British woollen industry! Similar series of payments appear for other pauper smallpox victims.

As vaccination spread so the disease became rarer until it disappeared entirely from Britain - so lifting a dreadful scourge from our ancestors' lives. People could now expect to go through life without this deadly and disfiguring disease hanging over them.

North Devon Journal 9.9.1999

73. The Shebbear bastards

The Child Support Agency has attracted its fair share of bad publicity yet its job of getting absent parents to help support their offspring is one that everyone would be in favour of - yet this idea is nothing new especially where the parents were unmarried. In the past our ancestors were just as determined to make the parents of illegitimate children pay for their offspring and not have the expense fall on the public purse. Every parish operated a simple system which can be illustrated by reference to a small collection of documents spanning the years 1799-1828 that survived in the Shebbear parish chest.

If an unmarried woman became pregnant she had, by law, to appear before a local magistrate either before or soon after the birth to name the father. Failure to do so could lead to a year in an unhealthy gaol. In addition midwives were ordered to demand the father's name whilst the poor mother was in labour - when she was at her most vulnerable. Where the woman went before the magistrate a printed form was used to record her answers.

Typical of these is 'The voluntary Examination of Sarah Griffin of Shebbear singlewoman' which was taken before J.Fortescue J.P. on the 22nd of July 1799. It begins 'This Examinant, on her Oath, doth decree, that she is with Child, and that the said Child is likely to be born a Bastard.' Our forefathers didn't believe in euphemisms at least where hard cash was concerned! Sarah went on to 'charge one John Smale' of Shebbear with 'having gotten the said Child on her Body. . . having had carnal knowledge of her Body on or about ten weeks ago.' She also added the important point that 'no other Person hath had carnal knowledge of her Body.' Sarah signed this declaration - or at least made her mark, being illiterate.

A slightly different document concerned Elizabeth Collacott, a widow of Meeth. She reports how she gave birth to a female child on 22nd July 1824 in Shebbear alleging that the father was one Christopher Folland. In this case a follow-up document records the magistrate's orders concerning both her and Christopher. He, as father, was to pay 15/- (75p) towards her 'lying-in' costs i.e. the costs of the midwife at the labour along with linen and other necessities. He was also to pay 1/6 (7.5p) a week until the child was old enough to support itself. Elizabeth was to pay 9d (4p) a week to the parish officers if she decided not to bring up the child herself.

These costs suggest her labour was straightforward as in another case, that of John Allen, a labourer of 'Bradford', and Mary Gay of Shebbear, the father was presented with a bill of £6.16.11 (£6.85) for 'lying-in' costs - a huge sum when one realises the average labourer's weekly wage was around 10/- (50p) at this date.Clearly this sum was too daunting for poor John as another document in this collection is an arrest warrant issued for him for non-payment of his dues. When it was made out he was said to owe £7.6.3 (£7.31) to the parish officers.

It is hard to say how common absconding by fathers was but it was well-known that a man could easily escape such payments by joining the Army or Navy where no embarrassing questions were asked and aliases were commonly used. The weekly payments would have gone to either the mother if she kept her child or to foster parents if the child were lucky. If it was unlucky the child would end up in the local workhouse until 'apprenticed' out at a very early age (as young as 5) to possibly cruel masters or mistresses from whom they often ran away.

Being born illegitimate in earlier centuries was not a good start to life. As these documents have shown the community certainly didn't put themselves out to welcome you or make your early life happy.

North Devon Journal 19.8.1999

74. Bad spelling and good accounts?

Today our government seems to be all about centralisation and the decline of local control. Whitehall dictates what our social services will be, it nominates quango members to rule us and even has the ultimate power of rate-capping local councils. It is somewhat disconcerting therefore to look back to the past century when such control was non-existent; indeed our ancestors would have disdained and actively fought any move by central government to curtail their local power. Every parish ran itself - and in so doing created its own records

Typical of these was the small community of Meshaw. Here all the, admittedly primitive, social services were run by just two men - the churchwarden and the Overseer of the Poor. Both offices were filled by annual election and in 1810 William Torrington became churchwarden and Roger Cock the Overseer. Their work would be unknown to us but for the survival of their accounts written in faded brown ink at the end of their year of service.

Income came from a series of 'Poor Rates' levied on their fellow parishioners that raised £90 and to this was added some £15.32 carried over from the year before. This sum went on a whole series of 'Disbursements' to the poor and needy. Thus Mary Cann received 40p a month - or just 10p a week to live on. Four other regular recipients are noted and between them they swallowed up nearly a quarter of the budget. One was Tamzin Griney who also got 5p when 'in distress'. Another payment was 50p 'for making of 2 Shirts for Robert Lee.'

Additionally 15p went to Elener Red 'for cleaning of Charity Leitheby' and making 'a Change' (of clothes) for her which suggests that poor Charity was disabled in some way. A 'Sailor with a pass' and 'two Sailors Wives with a pass' shared 5p. At this date if you were travelling and had a certificate from a magistrate you could legally claim small payments from the parishes you passed through to help you on your way. The largest single payment was £10.50 to a Mr.Adams 'about Lees Eyes' - evidently Georgian doctors who treated paupers did not give charitable reductions in their fees.

The following year John Foxford and James Loosemore took over the offices of warden and Overseer and their accounts are similar in content to those of their predecessors but their spelling is idiosyncratic to say the least. A man whose name is rendered as Robing Guney, for example, got 50p when 'in Destress' whilst the parish doctor's bill came to £3.17 for the 'thirst year'. Some 35p was spent buying 'two Pare of Stogins' for Robart Lee and another 9p went on 'two Ceeps' (caps) for 'Chirity Lithby' who we met earlier when her name was more recognisable. This lady also received a 'new Apern', a 'new shif' and a 'new jaket'. A little later in the year 9p went on 'mending sharts' (shirts) and 30p on a 'New par of shews' for Agness Lee. Shoe repairs were described with the term 'riting of Shews' or even 'sues'.

At this time postage on letters was paid by the recipient and this is duly noted - 'for Aletter from the poast 6d'. The expenses of the annual election of officers are also noted - 'for the expence of the miting 18/-' (90p) along with the cost of travelling to the nearest magistrate or justice of the peace to inform them of the names of those so chosen - 'for Going to iustes 1/6' (7.5p) The

'Nomination Warient' cost a further 12.5p. A final payment which seems excessive in the circumstances was 7.5p 'for writing of this Acount'.

They may not have been able to spell perhaps but they served their local community using money raised within the parish to help their fellow parishioners whilst using all their local knowledge to ensure it was spent wisely and fairly - not a bad system perhaps?

North Devon Journal 21.10.1999

75. The Overseers of Merton

The Napoleonic Wars saw Britain and its people undergo many traumatic changes. Men marched or sailed away to war many never to return - yet ordinary life still continued in its immemorial routines. From the small parish of Merton we can see glimpses of this from the records of the Overseer of the Poor for the years 1810 to 1814. These Overseers were responsible for collecting the poor rates from the richer parishioners and paying them out to the poor. The records they kept of these actions were recorded in a thin parchment covered volume now cared for in the North Devon Record Office.

The main entries for each month are the lists of payments to the parish poor. Thus in May 1810 £10.55 was distributed, with Mary Longram for example getting 60p and Ann Perkin 45p. Most of the recipients were women - probably widows too elderly to work for their living or deserted wives with hungry children to raise.

Alongside these recurring entries are lists of 'Extraordinaries' as they are termed. It is here that one can read the history of the parish and its people. Thus in July 1810 the 'Local Militia men' are paid £9.70. These part time soldiers were on permanent stand-by for the expected invasion by the French and their allies and presumably this money was their pay - which probably went to their wives and dependants. Notice that individual parishes paid this, thus saving the over-stretched central government from doing it! The following July saw a further £7.58 going to these men.

These payments were unusual, of course, most money, as ever, going towards the maintenance of the poor and the parish 'Poor House'. In August 1810 for example 12p went on 'Sweeping the Poor house Chimneys' whilst in December 6p was paid to George Madge 'for Cleaning the Poor house Gutter'. In October 1812 'Reparing the Poor House Oven' cost 52p. Such ovens were made of clay and were a famous product of the nearby Bideford potteries. One odd payment was the 22p paid to a Mr.Underhill for supplying three beds and 'Bundels of Straw' for the mattresses.

The Overseers also paid for the poor's clothes. Thus in January 1811 William Lewis was paid 'for making John Tricks Waiscott' whilst in September of that year 6p went to 'making Willm Staceys breeches' with a further 4p going on 'a Coat & Shift for E Guttrey'.

Periods of illness saw various payments usually for nursing. Elizabeth Handford seems to have been the parish nurse from the number of payments recorded. Thus she received 40p for 2 months 'attendance of Mary Madge' in 1811. Two years later she got £1.05 for 'Laying In' - possibly acting as midwife to a pauper mother. In July 1813 she earned 30p 'for Washing 6 in the Poor hous'. On one occasion she was paid 7p for 'cleaning Wollacots bed' plus 4p for '3 faggots of wood to dry the same'. Interestingly Elizabeth also appears in the list of paupers being supported by the Overseers.

Occasionally there are entries such as 'Willm Smale Burring Charge' of £1.51 in 1813 and 'Simon Phillipp's Burial fees' of £1.40 in 1811. They may have been paupers but their fellow parishioners ensured they got a decent burial.

Two other sets of entries are of interest in showing the wide range of work undertaken by the Overseers. In July 1811 Frances Leverton was given 25p being then in 'need'. At the same time 10p went on the 'Summons and her Oath' which refers to her reciting her life history before a magistrate in order to identify which parish should be looking after her. A further 35p went on obtaining a 'Removeable Order' and 25p 'for carrying her to Hatherleigh & carying of her home.'

Also in the same month 50p was spent 'For Drawing the List of Poppalation and Oath' and 12p for taking this list to Hatherleigh. These payments refer to the census of that year - only the second ever taken in Britain.

War and threats of invasion may have been the main topics of conversation in Merton in these early years of the nineteenth century but ordinary life still continued. Such records are not of course restricted to Merton, most parishes have similar ones - from which we can reconstruct portions at least of the ordinary lives of ordinary people.

North Devon Journal 27.1.2000

76. The poor's revenge

To be poor in the past was to be powerless. Landowners provided the magistrates, controlled the law and government and made very sure their rights came before those of their labourers. The poor only had one weapon - vandalism directed against their masters' property.

In this respect North Devon was no different to any other area of Britain. Records are scarce but a few of these acts of wanton damage were noted in the *London Gazette*, an official newspaper published by the Government and circulated to officials and law officers throughout the country.

The commonest version of this crime was arson and a case from Braunton in 1815 was typical. The *Gazette* entry reads 'Whereas it has been humbly represented unto His Royal Highness, the Prince Regent, that some evil disposed person or persons did on the evening of Thursday the 21st ultimo, between the hours of seven and eight, set fire to various ricks of corn, the property of Mr.John Hole of Saunton Court, within the parish of Braunton, in the County of Devon, which totally destroyed the same.'

The Prince Regent (George III was experiencing one of his periods of 'insanity') offered a free pardon to any accomplice who would give evidence against the actual arsonist. This was backed up by a reward of £210 made up of £100 from the West of England Fire and Life Insurance Company, £50 from

J.Cleveland the lord of the manor of Braunton, £50 from the victim John Hole and £10 from 'the Braunton Association' which was probably a group of local landowners who acted as a type of early Neighbourhood Watch scheme. This sum was an enormous attraction considering the average wage of a labourer at this date was roughly 40-50p - so that the reward represented about 8-10 years' wages!

Another attack was recorded from Chittlehampton in September 1822. In this one someone had 'wilfully and maliciously' burnt down three barns and a linhay on Brightly Farm plus two barns, a 'pound-house' and some barrels of cider on Winson Farm - both properties belonging to Lord Rolle. A royal pardon was once again on offer along with a reward of 100 guineas from Rolle for information leading to a conviction.

Other incidents are on record from Lapford in 1826, Knowstone in 1830 and Molland in 1832. This last concerned the destruction of 30 acres of woodland so this must have been a sizeable fire. At Knowstone a house occupied by a labourer Abraham Cockram was burnt down though this might have been an oblique attack on the rich landlord Robert Throckmorton who was also the owner of the woodland at Molland.

In 1803 Kingsnympton saw a horrific variation in this sequence of attacks when someone 'most cruelly and maliciously put to Death, by stabbing, a Mare, the property of James Hall of New Place.' Just over a week later a pregnant mare belonging to Hall was also killed. The reward in this instance was 200 guineas - clearly Georgian gentlemen valued their horses highly.

The oddest occurrence of this type of crime came in 1749 when four houses were burnt down in Northam. The notice in the *Gazette* adds that 'a Pile of Wood has been found in an empty House in the said Parish, which was supposed to have been laid there, with a Design to be in Readiness for setting Fire to other Houses.' It also noted the rather surprising belief 'that there is Reason to apprehend, that the Persons concerned therein intend to burn the Church.'

In this case a pardon was offered along with £20 from the local MP one Thomas Benson who is notorious in history as the man who had to flee the country after an insurance fraud went wrong in 1753 - obviously a case of setting a criminal to catch another.

Today people with grievances can go to court, join pressure groups or write to newspapers - a far more civilized way of doing things than the rather more robust actions of our ancestors!

North Devon Journal 8.10.1998

77. The *Cave and Lundy Review*

The Cave and Lundy Review consists of twelve issues of a literary magazine published in Barnstaple over the period January 1824 to January 1825. It was one of a series of local journals produced around this date and like the others was produced anonymously. This may seem odd to us today but it was usual at this period when the cult of personality was not well developed.

From various references within the text it seems that the magazine sprang from a group of local people who met at Saunton from 1822 on and read each other their literary productions. These writings and drawings were passed around the group in manuscript and the *Review* seems to have been undertaken in order to preserve these essays and poems in a more permanent form.

J.R.Chanter, writing in 1866, noted that it was produced 'under the editorship and management of a club of literary gentlemen, of whom the most prominent was Dr.Morgan.' In the absence of any more definite evidence this would appear to have been Dr.James Gordon Morgan who was living and carrying on his calling as a 'Physician' from Vicarage House in 1824. This was probably what is now the dental surgery at the end of Vicarage Street. That he was a medical doctor might be inferred from the long article in support of the then new North Devon Infirmary in the May edition of the magazine.

One might also speculate, given his surname and the large number of references to South Wales that he originated from that area. Indeed a poem in the September edition might well be an autobiographical sketch. That the editor wasn't totally committed to maintaining his anonymity was shown when he wrote,

'As to the person or office of Editor we cannot bring ourselves to gratify mere vulgar curiosity, but if any person qualified to ask the question, will put it to the Editor, through the Printer, such person may rely on every satisfaction.' Who the other contributors were is now impossible to discover as all we have today are their pseudonyms as listed in the final issue.

Whatever their names they were very aware of their rivals as references to them occur in some profusion. Thus the first number sees a reference to the *Miscellany* and a later poem refers to all four of North Devon's Regency publications - the *Goose*, the *Miscellany*, the *Gossip* and the *Review*. The *Barnstaple Miscellany* was first published in October 1823 by a group of local men and, as its name suggests, contained a variety of pieces of poetry, stories and local news. It was followed by *The Gossip* in December 1823 but this only lasted 3 issues. In January 1824 appeared both *The Review* and *The Universal Medley* but again the latter only lasted 3 issues before amalgamating with the *Miscellany* which was renamed *The North Devon Miscellany*. About the same time was published *The Crackling Goose* which was designed as a satire on a recently published long poem which, unsurprisingly, only lasted 2 issues. Clearly the *Review* was part of a marked flowering of local literary talent.

The editor of the *Review* had himself contributed to the *Miscellany* but this didn't stop him having a satirical sideswipe at it though he is much kinder to the infant *North Devon Journal* newspaper which first appeared in July 1824. The editor wrote 'Good luck to the *Journal* say we', reckoning the first issue 'particularly well got up.'

Why the *Review* finished is not explained though there are two clues in the text. In April it is noted that two of the local publications, the *Miscellany* and the *Gossip* had joined together suggesting that the market couldn't support so many literary productions. In August the editor notes a reduction in the price of the *Review* from 1/- (5p) which might indicate that his publication was too expensive for its audience.

Intriguingly as the Barnstaple periodicals came to an end so a Bideford one began production if we are to judge from the long (and critical) notice of it in the December *Review*. This issue was the final appearance of the *Review* itself yet the article on *'The last Revel at the Cave'* gives no reason for its cessation - perhaps the editor wearied of producing an average of 40 pages of material each month? Whatever the reason we can be grateful that he and his helpers persevered for a year and have left us a wonderfully entertaining collection of literary and historical pieces. Readers wishing to see the magazine for themselves will find a complete run in the North Devon Athenaeum.

78. Devon wrestlers

In the past 'Devon wrestling' was a well-known sport in the West Country boasting its own style and champions. A description of one match held in Ilfracombe is typical.

One man paraded the town with six silver spoons tied around his hat. Arriving at the church he placed the hat on one of the lamp standards as a challenge to all-comers. Any challenger would toss his hat into the makeshift ring constructed on the local 'green'. After drinking a glass of beer each the two wrestlers would put on 'loose coats of duck, one bearing the device of a black fighting cock and the other that of a red bird.'

Thus dressed they stepped into the ring and tried to grab the coat of their opponent and then 'kick each other's shins as hard as they could.' Devon wrestling wasn't for the faint-hearted - especially when one considers that hob-nailed boots were worn for the contest! Apparently some wrestlers protected their shins with pads made of horn and leather but 'others scorned such things.'

If a man was kicked to the ground he lost that round whilst the victor was he who could 'throw' three men. If three were thrown the victor was awarded the 6 spoons, if two were defeated he got 4 spoons and so on.

Records are fairly scarce although there are accounts from Bickington in 1824, Lynton in 1827, Appledore in 1832, Berrynarbor in 1836 and Kentisbury in 1849. These were small village meetings, larger events being concentrated in the towns. South Molton saw the Devon champion Abraham Cann visit in 1825, whilst a contest in 1827 saw 44 different matches. This latter meeting was even celebrated by a poem written by a keen follower of the sport. Another match in the town in 1842 had £30 worth of prizes on offer - at a time when the average labourer only earned 10/- (50p) a week.

Another important centre was Barnstaple where, for example, matches took place on at least 8 occasions between 1827-49 most of these occurring during the Fair Week. Sites seem to have been variable; in 1830 the matches took place at the Newington Inn in the Derby area of the town. A contemporary advertisement noted that 'A Spacious Booth will be erected and every accommodation provided.' Admission to the 'Booth' was 1/- (5p) whilst spectators around the 'Ring' only paid half that. Twelve years later the matches were being held 'in a field at the head of Bearstreet' whilst in 1843 there is mention of 'the wrestling ring near Barnstaple Bridge' - a site also used in 1849.

Champions were celebrities and their marriages, death and brushes with the law were noted by the *Journal*. Thus when John Flower died, aged 46, at Chulmleigh he was recorded as the greatest prizewinner ever known and famous for never cheating. The marriage of George Paige of Sheepwash was recorded in 1843 as was the fact that he was a 'celebrated wrestler'.

Not everyone thought the sport acceptable. In 1827 a J.Barry wrote to the *Journal* attacking wrestling and backing their argument with biblical quotes. An editorial comment in an issue of the *Journal* in 1845 began, 'We are sorry to announce that the brutal and disgraceful sport of wrestling has been again attempted in this town' whilst a month later the sport was labelled a 'brutal pastime'.

Brutality was certainly evident. In 1827 for example William Elworthy of Torrington broke his leg in a match as did William Parkin of Barnstaple in 1837. Three years later at Ilfracombe a wrestler called Colking threw his opponent Jewell 'with so much violence to the ground, that his neck was dislocated and his back dreadfully injured, so that his life for some time despaired of, and he now lies in a precarious state.' At one match in Braunton in 1832 John Vodden had his collarbone broken by William Challacombe following which John tried, unsuccessfully, to sue William for assault! The worst case of all occurred at

Bratton Fleming in 1843 when Henry Phillips, aged 22, died of wounds he received in the ring.

The sport seems to have died out completely in the second half of the nineteenth century - a victim, perhaps, of the urge to 'clean up' the rough manners of the working class by church-inspired middle class meddlers. How many people today, however, would want to stand in a ring trading kicks to their shins? Very few I suspect!

North Devon Journal 11.2.1999

79. The Lynton wrestlers

The older we get the more our memories mean to us. In July 1912, Lynton octogenarian, Mr.W.Hooper, set down a few scattered incidents he could remember from his own long life. They were printed in the *Journal* not surprisingly as 'for fifty years he had not missed seeing weekly a copy of the *North Devon Journal*'.

The anonymous reporter who took down his reminiscences talks of Mr.Hooper as being 'gifted with illimitable colloquial eloquence and an unfailing fund of humour.' He had apparently studied 'politics closely, has opinions of his own on politics as on everything else, which he expresses with refreshing force and fire.'

Hooper had been born around 1830, his father having been tenant at Wingate Farm, Countisbury, where their landlord was the Reverend W.S.Halliday. To put this period into context one of Hooper's first memories was from 1841 when Edward, Prince of Wales was born. Mr.Halliday gave a treat to his parishioners which Hooper described as 'a fine old time' adding, 'The great thing at this affair was a tea-drinking contest, in which there was great rivalry among the old ladies' as to which of them could drink the hottest cup of tea in the shortest time. On this occasion old Sally Groves won a popular victory.

Simple pleasures but not all was happiness. Hooper could clearly recall the 'Hungry Forties' (the 1840s) 'when the people lived on barley bread and bacon' - when they could get it - and when tea 'could not be procured at under 4/- (20p) per lb.' This was when average wages were roughly 8/- (40p) a week, so the hardship can be imagined.

If these were unhappy times happier were Hooper's memories of the Lynton Revel - always held on the first Sunday after Mid-Summer Day. The high spot of this village fair was the wrestling. We read that on 'Sunday the man (in charge) would wear a number of silver spoons, which were the prizes to be competed for, in a top hat. Thus attired, he marched to the church, the admired of all beholders. When he got to church he took the hat off, and it was hung prominently in the gallery, where everybody could see it.'

The wrestling match took place the next day this being 'a sight worth seeing'. These matches sound savage affairs, especially when we read, 'A feature of the wrestling matches was the effective use which was made of the legs. A really good wrestler had to be a really good kicker, and he had himself to have legs tough as iron.'

Hardly what we see today on our televisions! One competitor from Challacombe decided to protect his shins with a layer of padding under his trouser leg (evidently they fought in clothes). He was only found out when 'in response to a particularly brilliant effort on the part of his opponent. The bottom of his trouser legs split, the stuffing fell out, and the luckless young fellow fled amid the laughter of the delighted crowd.'

We could wish that Mr.Hooper had recorded more than just these few fleeting glimpses into early Victorian North Devon - but how revealing are those he did set down.

North Devon Journal-Herald 25.4.1985

80. Worked to death in the South Molton Workhouse

In December 1843 an inquest was held in North Molton into the death of Elizabeth Tidboald a 12 year old pauper of that parish. At this hearing allegations of mistreatment were made against the medical officer of South Molton Workhouse where she had been staying. It was said that she had been literally worked to death. So serious were they that a grandly titled Poor Law Commissioner came down from London to look into them

At the public inquiry into the case the first witness was James Cole the Relieving Officer of the area served by the South Molton Workhouse. It was his duty to examine paupers and record their details. He had first seen Elizabeth in September when she was suffering with a 'diseased heart'. He had given her 10p plus a loaf of bread each week for seven weeks but a dispute had arisen whether North Molton or Witheridge were liable for her upkeep and she was sent to the Workhouse to have her case examined. Prior to her journey he had asked Mr.Flexman the parish doctor to check if she was well enough to travel to South Molton and this was done although the doctor noted 'she must be carefully removed, as she was in a very precarious state.'

Robert Jewell, the Governor of the Workhouse, then recounted how Elizabeth had arrived into his care. He had ordered the nurse to help Elizabeth change her clothes and the nurse later reported that the girl was 'very thin and emaciated, nothing but skin and bones.' The following day he had her removed to the Sick Ward as 'she looked very ill.' Four days later Elizabeth's mother turned up and took her daughter home with her where she died 8 days later.

This account was backed up by the Workhouse matron Margaretta Jewell who gave details of Elizabeth's failure to eat much whilst under her care. On her first day she ate neither breakfast nor tea which was bacon and bread. When the matron had asked if she didn't like bacon she got the reply 'she liked it very well but it was too gross for her stomach.' The Workhouse surgeon Mr Cutcliffe checked her and said 'I don't see much the matter with her' reckoning she could be put to 'light work' helping to look after the children in the nursery. The matron added that every day she asked Elizabeth how she felt and every time got the answer 'Just the same'. Her assistant Elizabeth Herley corroborated all this noting that the only work the girl did whilst in the Workhouse was to nurse a 6 month old child for a few hours each day.

The Workhouse schoolmistress Sarah Widgery next appeared but added little new to the account merely stating that Elizabeth 'seemed short in her breath while she was in the house, but made no complaint.' The surgeon John Cutcliffe then gave his evidence which only repeated what had been heard before.

The final witness was James Flexman the parish doctor of North Molton. He had been treating Elizabeth since April 1843 for a diseased heart both as a private and a 'parish' patient. At the post-mortem which he carried out it was clear that she had died of a ruptured vein in her heart. Asked if the work she had been put to in the Workhouse could have caused her death he replied 'Certainly not' which appears odd in the light of what was said a few minutes later.

Rather bizarrely it emerged that it was he who had asked for an inquest on the grounds that Elizabeth had been killed by overwork in the Workhouse! Cross-examination further revealed that he and Dr.Cutcliffe had not been on speaking terms for many years and indeed it became clear that Flexman had spread rumours about Elizabeth's treatment in order to smear his fellow practitioner's good name. The reason for this appears to have been twofold, one, Flexman hated Cutcliffe and two, he got a guinea for attending an inquest and two guineas for carrying out a post-mortem!

The report on the hearing ended with the *Journal* writer remarking that 'the case was a new edition of "Much ado about nothing" and that the disclosures made exhibited the conduct of the officers of the Workhouse very far otherwise than in a discreditable light.' On that note the case of poor Elizabeth and her feuding doctors disappears from the record - a short and sad life consigned to the yellowing pages of old newspapers.
North Devon Journal 6.5.1999

81. The worthless wife
Prior to 1857 divorce was a virtual impossibility for most people in Britain. For the poor especially the only way of ending an unhappy marriage was desertion - yet this carried legal penalties if one of the partners decided to pursue the other. An unusual example of this came before the Barnstaple magistrates' bench in May 1850.

Elizabeth Beer, wife of Joel a shoemaker of Exeter, appeared to ask the court for 'protection' from her husband. They had been married 19 years previously - her husband then being penniless. Although they had five children she alleged that since marrying him 'she had been subjected to a series of brutal treatments at his hands.' This had got steadily worse until she had to go before the Exeter magistrates and have him bound over to keep the peace for twelve months.

Six months before she had left him, eventually ending up in Barnstaple. He had tracked her down, however, to her lodgings and 'made use of the most violent threats.' She, being terrified, agreed to go back to Exeter with him but only two miles out of Barnstaple he had 'beaten and ill-treated her in a shocking manner.' As proof she showed her badly bruised arms - which elicited the sympathy of all the spectators in the court.

Joel Beer was then called to explain himself - and he described a very different series of events. He began by admitting that he had been penniless when he married Elizabeth but 'by dint of industry he was soon gaining a comfortable subsistence, having under his employ as many as sixteen journeymen.' Sadly his 'wife's conduct underwent a strange alteration' and she began associating with bad companions and drinking heavily. Indeed she spent so much on drink that he eventually became a bankrupt.

Six months before she had run off with another man leaving him to look after their children. Although he tried he could hear nothing of her until the week previous when he was told she was in Barnstaple. He immediately walked from Exeter to try and persuade her to come home with him.

This he managed to do and they set off but after a very short time and 'under the influence of liquor' she turned on him 'and abused him in every possible way' until his self-control broke and he hit her. He added that the landlady at her lodgings had heard Elizabeth twice threaten to knife him. The magistrates immediately summoned this landlady who agreed to the truth of Joel's evidence adding that Elizabeth 'had been living at her house as a married woman with the other man in question for five weeks past.' This damning corroboration meant that the magistrates immediately refused to grant Elizabeth any protection. Joel then offered in open court to take her home saying 'as she had shared his prosperity, she ought now to share his adversity, and that if she would return with him, all might be well again.'

Elizabeth we are told 'indignantly refused' and the Mayor of Barnstaple, who was the chief magistrate, gave the crushing reply to Joel 'that such a worthless woman did not deserve such kindness, and was not worth conveying home.' Not very politically correct perhaps but he was probably only saying what most of those present thought - hard justice for a hard case.
North Devon Journal 2.12.1999

82. The poisoning of a baby

Childcare is as subject to fashion as anything else. The old Victorian adage 'children should be seen but not heard' has given way to the child centred approach of the late twentieth century. It could be argued that this is a retrograde step but one absolute advance is in children's medicine - as a case from 1850 shows.

In that year a 23 year old woman named Mrs.Brent of Union Street, Derby in Barnstaple gave birth to a boy whom she christened Charles. He was a fractious baby and she took the usual course taken by working class mothers at that date - she dosed him with 'a narcotic draught' to make him sleep. Unfortunately he died of its effects and as was then the habit an inquest was held by the coroner on the same day as his death.

At this the mother recounted how her six weeks old son 'was very cross, indeed there was no peace at all with him.' Previously when he had been like this she had given him a proprietary mixture called Godfrey's Cordial and she decided to go to the chemist Mr.Tatham for some. On the way there she met Ellen Cawsey who told her that 'Mr.Weeks' stuff was much better' and so she went to his shop and purchased one pennyworth of the medicine which was mixed up in front of her using 3 different ingredients by one of the chemist's assistants.

She returned home and gave Charles a spoonful after mixing it with warm water and sugar. He 'sucked it in readily'. Two hours later, however, he was sweating profusely and making strange noises in his throat. She sent for a Dr.Cooke but the baby died in a few hours.

Mr.Weeks then appeared and gave evidence that Mrs.Brent had asked him for 'something that would operate stronger' than the cordial she had used previously. He prepared her a mixture made up of twenty drops of opium and one teaspoonful of 'a simple syrup', the whole being topped up with dill water. The bottle held about six small teaspoonfuls of liquid. The inquest jury asked to see the bottle but were told that the child's father 'when aware that it had caused his child's death, had thrown it away in a passion.'

Dr.Cooke's evidence was then heard. He had been summoned by his assistant who had given the baby an emetic to clear its stomach he having recognised 'the effects of narcotic poison.' Mustard poultices were applied and a warm bath provided. The doctor also 'desired that every effort should be made to excite it [the child] in order that it might be roused from its state of lethargy.' All this was to no avail as the child had died in the early hours of that morning.

A juryman then intervened reckoning that 'One half of the children who are dosed with 'soothing syrup' or 'mother's quiet' do not survive one year.' This lead to the coroner calling Ellen Cawsey who brought along her bottle of Mr.Weeks' cordial. She claimed that she regularly used it and it kept her child asleep for three hours at a stretch and had never harmed it.

When asked if this was his preparation Weeks tasted it and 'at once declared that he had never prescribed such a thing in his life for any child' as it was roughly 50% pure opium. Ellen, however, insisted that one of his two assistants had made it up for her. For some unexplained reason neither of these two young men were called to give evidence - which, with the benefit of hindsight might well have cleared up some of the mysteries in this case.

Nevertheless the jury arrived at their obvious verdict - that Charles Brent 'died from the effects of an overdose of anodyne cordial.' They added the rider that 'great blame attaches to the party selling such description of medicine without proper labels being attached thereto.' They also severely censured the poor

mother 'for the careless manner in which the medicine was administered.' The coroner, after addressing her, brought the inquest to a close - a bureaucratic end to a very short life terminated so sadly and needlessly.
North Devon Journal 18.11.1999

83. Awakening to the unexpected

Over the years I have been reading old newspapers I have come across a fair number of odd headlines. None, however, have been quite so bizarre as the one which appeared in the *Journal* on 30 April 1857. This read 'A Man's Leg Dropping Off In His Sleep'. Who could resist reading an article introduced by this phrase?

Actually the start of the piece is almost as strange as the title as it begins with a masterly example of understatement, 'It must create a very curious and not very pleasant sensation for a man to find in the morning. . . one of his limbs. . . lying, when he awakes, in everlasting separation from him at his side.' No-one is going to disagree with that I feel sure.

The unfortunate sufferer was one George Slewman then aged 89 and living in Bideford. Described as being in good general health with 'intellect unimpared' he had fallen victim to the ravages of age and 'been a bed-lier for the last seven years.' In late 1855 he began feeling a pain in his heel and his wife, thinking it was rheumatism, gave him a worsted stocking to keep his foot warm. Over the next three weeks, however, his lower leg and foot became very swollen and a liquid began oozing out. Within a few days the skin in the affected area first turned brown and then 'perfectly black' the skin being described as 'hard as horn.' The leg remained in this state for thirteen months without any wasting or further change occurring.

Then one night whilst George was asleep he suddenly awoke 'with a convulsive start' to find that this blackened leg 'had actually dropped from his body.' The doctor, T.L.Pridham, who was called in to view this amazing case reckoned that his patient's sudden awakening had 'snapped the decayed bone asunder' and caused the useless leg to drop off. There was no bleeding and the stump looked as clean as if a surgical operation had been carried out. Apparently George kept the leg which 'was exhibited as a curiosity to any friend who might call' - which suggests he had some fairly morbid not to say strong stomached acquaintances!

The article ended with a discussion of how such 'mortifications' usually ended in death but George was said to have such a powerful constitution that he both survived and indeed triumphed over his illness as, after losing his leg, he was 'now in comparatively good health.'

George had been born in Horwood and worked for most of his life as an agricultural labourer. His wife, to whom he had been married 66 years, was his nurse and she came in for praise from Dr.Pridham for her dedication to keeping her husband healthy.

Examination of the records of the Registrar General shows that George was dead within a year which was not perhaps surprising though as he was 90 when he died - and given the history of his leg - he clearly must have been a tough old character.
North Devon Journal 1.4.1999

84. The bad loser of Instow

When we want some building work done today we are always told to obtain a range of estimates in order to get the best value for our money. Obviously the unsuccessful tenderers are disappointed but few seem to have taken their disappointment to heart as much as one Robert Pinkham.

He was a mason from Instow who, in 1857, put in one of a series of tenders to build a wall for C.Palmer, a prominent landowner in the village. The contract went to another local mason Samuel Vanstone who began work soon after being awarded the job whilst Pinkham was employed by Palmer as a general labourer - at a much lower rate of pay than Vanstone.

The wall rapidly began to take shape but heavy rain caused Vanstone to give up early one day and after covering the unfinished section with boards to protect it he went home. Coming back the next morning to finish the job he found 'three perches knocked down' - evidently done wilfully and maliciously. Looking round he found an iron bar which had probably been used to do the damage, along with some footprints 'of a peculiar kind' which were identified as having being made by Pinkham.

The latter was arrested and taken to court to answer the charge of criminal damage even though the only evidence against him was circumstantial. Here Vanstone's evidence about the peculiarity of the footprint was seriously questioned and Pinkham's boots were produced. It was argued that in fact that the footprint made by these boots 'did not appear to have anything very uncommon about it' and certainly did not prove that their owner had been anywhere near the wall on the night it was being vandalised. Interestingly Vanstone had recognised the footprints after seeing 'the bottom of defendant's boot when he was creeping over the rafters at work.'

After some close cross-examination, however, Pinkham had to admit that on the day in question after finishing work he had gone to see how the wall was progressing and that he had probably left footprints around the area. Realising that this showed him in an obviously bad light he began to bluster claiming that he was blamed for everything that went wrong in Instow. Indeed 'he believed if a house were to fall down while he was here before the court, he would be sure to be accused of knocking it down.'

He then offered an account of his movements on the night the damage was done. He had gone home after work, 'killed a pig for one of his neighbours' and stayed for supper with them until 10 p.m. - although, tellingly, he didn't call this neighbour as a witness.

The magistrates hearing the case didn't take long to make up their minds after giving 'their best attention to the evidence produced.' Although there was a very strong suspicion against Pinkham they needed better proof of his guilt than some footprints and, with some obvious reluctance, they dismissed the case. It is probably safe to assume that Pinkham was never asked again to tender for work by local people in Instow who knew what might happen if he wasn't awarded the contract!

North Devon Journal 14.10.1999

85. Penny readings in Victorian Bideford

Our Victorian ancestors, not content with introducing compulsory education for all, also believed strongly in the benefits of night school. In North Devon these were generally organised by the middle class for the benefit of the working class and often took the form of 'Penny Readings'. At these events, admission one penny, relatively well educated men would read sections of uplifting prose or poetry to the workers who had come to be educated and entertained at the same time - which might strike us as condescending but was an accepted way of life for most.

Bideford began such 'Readings' in the late 1860s but by March 1868 they were not going quite as planned. In a letter to the *Journal* 'A Christian' began by declaring that 'the early promoters of Penny Readings, were activated by a desire to improve mentally and morally the condition of the people, and to bring about in their respective localities a sound, elevating, social good.' Unfortunately the writer had gone to several such events in Bideford Town Hall where the sheer numbers present prevented his walking out and so he had 'to listen to an amount of nonsense and at other times to hear the name of the Deity bellowed forth so irreverently by some of the readers as if we had been beyond the confines of a Christian land!' When he approached the organiser of the Readings to complain - and demand that only serious and useful talks be staged - he was met with 'a pitiable laugh' followed by the assertion that 'nothing serious would do.'

The truth of this was shown in a contemporary article on the Bideford 'Readings'. Apparently there had been 'a direct attempt to annoy every reader (by coughing, talking, and stomping) who has taken any subject of interest, or of an elevating tendency.' A Thomas Pynsent had been 'very badly treated' whilst the organiser J.Harafane Dowsett 'received a snubbing'. George Whitaker tried to read his lachrymose piece titled 'The Female Convict' but 'was not allowed even to be heard, some of the finest and most touching sentences being received with shouts of laughter.'

Whitaker, however, was not to be beaten and returned the next week to read a piece entitled 'The Aged Mother'. Before he began the chairman 'impressed upon the audience the necessity of giving every reader a fair hearing.' Whitaker followed this up 'with a brief and cutting prologue on the treatment he received at a former reading' - and suitably chastised his audience fell quiet. He then began reading 'The Aged Mother' but this turned out in actual fact to be 'Old Mother Hubbard' - his way of making a sarcastic comment on the level of intelligence of his listeners!

According to the *Journal*'s report the crowd were 'fairly taken aback'. The first verse 'was read in profound silence' but was followed by huge cheering and cries of 'Well done' and 'Bravo'. Whitaker then 'coolly told the audience that, as the work could be got for a ha'penny, they could buy it and read the remainder for themselves' before leaving abruptly - and before the audience remembered they had paid a penny to hear a poem they could have bought for a halfpenny!

Dowsett the organiser tried to claim that the *Journal*'s account was 'utterly false' but the editor merely answered 'We have too much confidence in our correspondent, to doubt the truthfulness of his communication to this *Journal*.' It is clear from this that not all Victorian workers were quite as subservient as we might believe - and not all Victorian 'do-gooders' were quite so po-faced as we assume.

86. Death at Playford Mills

Inquests, by their very nature, are sad occasions. Rarely are they as shocking, however, as one held in Barnstaple in May 1871 to inquire into the death of John Smith who perished in an industrial accident.

The evidence presented to the Coroner was straightforward. The dead man had been employed at the Playford Paper Mills near Barnstaple for just three weeks by the owner Mr.Abbot to superintend the running of the boilers in the factory. These boilers had a safety device fitted to check whether all the steam in them had condensed out before they were opened. On this occasion it seems that Smith had arrived early (at 3 a.m!) and opened one without first checking. The consequent blast as the pressurised steam escaped threw him backwards with such violence that he fractured his skull whilst the steam scalded him all over his body.

Knocked unconscious at first Smith revived, staggered out into the road and stumbled down to Pilton where at 4 a.m. his groans awoke Christopher Vickery who was caretaker at the local reservoir. Looking out of his window Christopher asked Smith what was wrong and got the reply, 'I've scalded myself just to death.' Dressing quickly he rushed to help the injured man who 'appeared to be suffering very much.'

After being supported a little way Smith fell down and said he could go no further so Christopher ran to the house of a Mr.Leverton, woke him up and asked to borrow his donkey and cart to transport Smith to hospital. To his anguish Leverton refused saying 'he must attend to his business.'

Shocked Christopher ran on to the house of Mr.Abbot the mill owner who immediately dressed and went back with Christopher to help his injured employee. On the way they met William Harding who was loading a cart. Asking him to help move Smith he also refused saying 'he could not leave his work.'

Whilst this occurred Smith himself had woken a man called George Huxtable who ran to help him and sent another to ask at Mr.Ireland's nursery garden if they could borrow a cart - but they too refused. Luckily a passing milkman called John Allen wasn't so cold-hearted and he took the victim to hospital where, as he was undressed, his scalded skin peeled off in large quantities. Mr.Cooke, the house surgeon, recounted how his patient died of shock very shortly after arrival.

Following the evidence the Coroner summed up saying that the real reason for Smith's death would never be known there being no witnesses to the event. He did comment, however, on 'the inhumanity of those persons who were asked to help that poor creature suffering as he was'. Indeed 'he hoped to have few instances of such inhumanity, which made the blood curdle in their veins.'

He continued in this way for some time and then asked the jury to give their verdict which, needless to say, was 'Accidental Death' to which was added the rider, 'The jury wishes to express its strong sense of disapprobation at the unfeeling manner in

which the parties acted in refusing to help the deceased to the Infirmary.' One juryman added his personal comment saying 'I hope they will be held up to public indignation and to scorn.' So ended this heart-rending case which to many seemed a horrifying re-enactment of the story of the Good Samaritan and which, doubtless, made pariahs of Leverton, Harding and Ireland.
North Devon Journal 30.9.1999

87. Mayhem in Marwood

Everyone, it is said, should make a will - if only to avoid family squabbles following our death. In the past it has been estimated that only 1 in 10 people made a will with the rest dying intestate i.e. not having made one. Even when wills were drawn up, however, family disputes could still develop - as is shown by a case from Marwood.

John Lamprey was the freehold owner of an estate called Blakewell in the parish which, when he died, passed to his widow. She died around Christmas 1872 and her nephew, John Boyle Rock of Pilton, expected to inherit the estate as her closest surviving relative. Mrs.Lamprey, however, had evidently had different ideas and left it in her will to her grandniece Mrs.Miller nee Carder of Whiddon Farm in Marwood.

Rock was so upset at losing what he regarded as his rightful inheritance that he disputed the will in the courts but the judges found in Mrs.Miller's favour. Having lost the legal battle Rock turned to illegal means.

The property had been let to a Mr.Seage and he and Mrs.Miller had asked one of the farm labourers to live in the farm whilst she decided what to do with it - this was also to publicly assert her right to the property. Rock's first action was to hire a man who acted as 'a scout near the premises' all one week to ascertain the labourer's movements and see when the property was empty.

Knowing that the labourer would be absent on the Saturday evening Rock turned up with five hired toughs in tow and forced his way in announcing 'that the property was his and he meant to keep it.' The tenant Mr.Seage soon heard what had happened and demanded 'that Mr.Rock should turn out' which, not surprisingly, 'he refused to do.'

Seage and Mrs.Miller then sent a man in to deliver a written demand that Rock leave with the threat that 'they would be dealt with as being there for some unlawful purpose' if they refused - which, of course, they did. The ousted parties then hired a local builder bearing the wonderful name Lemon Kellaway along with twenty stout labourers from Barnstaple and Marwood. This force 'came shouting to the top of their voices to lay siege to the place.' After rushing through the yard they forced the main door with a crowbar.

As the door gave way Rock leapt at them and hit the first man he encountered 'a heavy blow on the head' with an iron bar. This unfortunate man, called Ballment, 'sustained a flesh wound two inches long, severe but not dangerous.' This cowardly attack infuriated the besiegers who seized Rock and 'amidst fierce cries of 'Murder!' dragged him out of the house and hurled him into the road. Seeing this, the rest of Rock's men hurriedly left. Only two women stayed behind, one of whom 'made a show of fight with a hammer' but she was soon disarmed and kicked out. In the house the victors found razors and other weapons which had been laid out in expectation of a bloody fight. Clearly our ancestors took their property disputes very seriously.

The story didn't end there, however, as a few days later Rock returned and cut down a number of trees on the estate and took them away to Barnstaple as a crude means of asserting his ownership. This led to a court case which he lost. Nothing daunted a month later he paid a bailiff to sieze nine cows belonging to Seage which were taken to Pilton.

This was the last straw and Seage and Mrs.Miller charged Rock and seven of his hired men with conspiracy. After two inconclusive court hearings the case finally came to a head in March 1874. Here Mrs.Miller's lawyer said that 'there was no desire to punish the defendants', all that was wanted was 'to prevent a recurrence of what had taken place.'

The judge announced that he found Rock guilty of conspiracy and set a recognizance of £500 on him to leave Mrs.Miller and Seage alone. This sum is the equivalent of about £50,000 today.

The seven other men in the case were similarly bound over in sums of £50 each - thus bringing this long and complex case to an end. Stirring times and not the usual behaviour we might expect of Victorian families.

North Devon Journal 3.2.2000

88. Freemasons, rent and roughs

Freemasons are a secretive body who have rarely appeared in the full glow of publicity - but in June 1873 the Barnstaple Lodge went through an extremely public and embarrassing episode.

Some 18 months previously one of their members, Henry Gliddon, had been running a billiard hall in Cross Street. As he only had one table his income must have been limited - so he took to selling beer to the players. Unfortunately he over-looked the need for a licence and the local Excise authorities prosecuted him. At court he was found guilty and heavily fined. As he had little money his billiard table was seized under a distress warrant and sold by the court bailiffs.

Penniless, he appealed to his fellow masons who offered to house him and his family temporarily in a cottage adjoining their Lodge until he got back on his feet. At this date the Lodge was housed in Queen Anne's Walk and the cottage appears to have been behind it.

The Gliddon family moved in and liked it so much that they refused to go when the masons subsequently let it to a paying tenant. Mr.Ffinch a local solicitor served 'repeated notices' to them to quit but they refused point-blank to leave. As the *Journal* report puts it, 'Neither persuasion, threats, nor the offer of a bribe could get Gliddon and his family to budge.'

Faced with this intransigence the masons decided to ignore the law and try direct action. They paid a local chimney sweep called Pavey to lead an assault on the cottage one Saturday afternoon. It was he who, at the head of a group of men hired by the masons, first forced his way through the door.

No sooner was he inside, however, than he was attacked by the family notably Mrs.Gliddon, 'who used her hands rather freely and evidently with a more vicious intention than that of getting the soot off Pavey's face.' After being roughed up the unfortunate sweep was thrown out into the street 'amidst the shouts and laughter' of a crowd numbering 400 who had collected to see the fun.

The hired men then smashed all the panes of glass in the cottage and poured 'ammonia water' in 'for the purpose of stinking them out.' Unfortunately, although the stench was overpowering, it didn't do the job.

A 'storming party' was next formed who used 'masons' large stone hammers' to break the door down. The door, however, was 'a substantial one' and they only succeeded in smashing through the door panels. A few of the besiegers then stuck their heads through the holes to try and reach the lock inside. The Gliddons immediately hurled buckets of cold water over them and drove them off.

Nothing daunted the men continued to batter the door and when it eventually gave way rushed in. The Gliddons, recognising the game was up thereupon surrendered and left with their goods and chattels. Bizarrely, whilst this was going on, the Town Crier was marching up and down amongst the crowd publicising a 'lecture on emigration' being delivered that evening in the town.

Once the Gliddons were out the Freemasons made good the damage and let the new occupiers in. Their use of Queen Anne's Walk lasted another 60 years, they only finally leaving in 1933 for their new home in Trafalgar Lawn. Doubtless they weren't quite so generous to fellow members who had fallen on hard times in the future!

North Devon Journal 28.10.1999

89. Suicide at the Workhouse

The treatment of mentally ill people is still a very contentious issue in our society, yet we do show a great deal more understanding than our ancestors ever did - as shown by a sad case from March 1874. It was then that 65 year old Dorothy Quick 'a quiet and inoffensive woman' from Croyde was taken to Barnstaple Workhouse as she 'appeared to be under some delusion about religion.' After 8 days there she hanged herself - and an inquest was held which displayed Victorian attitudes to mental health well.

Held before the borough coroner R.Bencraft 'a respectable jury' under a Mr.Cummins was sworn in to hear the evidence. The first witness was Ellen Squire an inmate of the Workhouse who had known Dorothy for some 8 years. Ellen had been in the sick ward and noted how Dorothy 'seemed to be in a very good bodily health', indeed she had a good appetite and had no difficulty getting about. Her only 'illness' seemed to be an obsession that 'she could not be saved, but must go to hell'. Ellen used to ask her 'Well, Dorothy, have you done any great crime?', and receive the answer 'No' which prompted Ellen to say 'she should not give up in that way'.

Sadly, however, Ellen then went on to recount how she had discovered her friend sitting on a toilet seat with a rolled up handkerchief around her neck, the two ends being 'fastened to the crook of the window at her back'. Ellen immediately fetched the nurse and between them they took Ellen back to her bed but by the time Dr.Cook the Workhouse doctor arrived she was 'quite dead'.

The second witness was the nurse Maria Rowe who remembered how when Ellen entered the Workhouse 'she talked quite sensibly' asking Maria 'to take care of a shilling or two for her to buy tea and sugar with.' Initially Dr.Cook had suggested Ellen was 'out of her mind' but after examining her said 'he did not see much the matter with her.' The only hint that Ellen was mentally unbalanced came after Sunday chapel when she went straight to bed and when Maria asked what was wrong replied 'I am a lost sinner, and shall go to hell.' Maria comforted the woman and read to her 'and she seemed to be easier'. The nurse even had her moved into the less noisy sick ward so she would find it easier to sleep. On a less happy note Maria took away a penknife which Ellen claimed she had used in a previous suicide attempt.

The next witness was Dr.Cook who confirmed the nurse's evidence that he could find 'nothing amiss' with Ellen although he too had heard her say 'she was a lost sinner'. Unfortunately no-one had told him she had tried to commit suicide before but as a precaution he had ordered 'she should be watched' though this was more to gauge her state of mind than to prevent her killing herself.

Asked his opinion now he thought she must have been unbalanced though 'If they were to send every one in the Workhouse, who was temporarily of unsound mind to the Asylum, they would have to depopulate nearly half the Workhouse.' Indeed, and rather unnecessarily, he added 'Aged people were often temporarily wandering.' His rather casual attitude to mental illness was echoed by the Reverend H.J.Bull who remarked how sometimes paupers who were 'reported to be insane' had been sent to the County Asylum at Exminster but 'had been returned at the end of a day or two'.

Coroner Bencraft then summed up the evidence and the jury rapidly returned a verdict that Ellen had 'strangled herself' being 'of unsound mind' - with the rider that 'they considered every possible attention had been shewn the deceased, and that blame in no way attached to the Union authorities.' On that note Ellen disappears from history an 'inoffensive' old lady whose religious mania got the better of her - a sad story that we can only hope would not happen today.

North Devon Journal 26.11.1998

90. The Yellow Pages of time

As a local historian it is intriguing to speculate which of our present records will be of most use to historians in the future. Clearly our newspapers, diaries and photographs will be as highly valued as Victorian ones are today. But what of our 'Yellow Pages'? This may seem a strange source to quote but their nineteenth century equivalent, the trade directories, are now scarce and expensive survivals. Various companies issued them e.g. *Kelly's* and *White's* and they run from the late eighteenth century up until the 1960s.

The '*Devon*' volume issued by *White's* in 1879 is typical of them all as is the seven page entry for South Molton. It begins with a short history and statistical review of the town and then moves on to list the twelve strong Town Council under the Mayor John Galliford. Various other officers are listed as are the officials staffing the Workhouse and Courts. Details of churches, chapels, schools, charities, postal arrangements and banks then follow.

The Directory then launches into a four page alphabetical listing of all the gentry and tradespeople then living in the town. This was the main selling point of the Directory of course making it essential to the multitudes of nineteenth century travelling salesmen. Their richest target, the gentry, are not actually identified as such but they have no trade listed and the men bear the honorific 'Mr.' in front of their names unlike their working counterparts. Some fifty seven are named.

Just below these in the social structure were the professionals such as the bank manager William Brewer and solicitor Russell Riccard, this latter gentleman also being the town clerk and Superintendant Registrar. This mix of jobs was nothing unusual for this period in small towns such as South Molton. Thus William Manning identified himself as an auctioneer, appraiser, grocer, tea dealer, postal agent, insurance agent and Borough Sanitary Inspector which is an intriguing mix.

Such men could have sent their children to a variety of schools. Most important was the Free School founded in 1682 by Hugh Squier. Others included the Blue Coat, the National, the British, the 'Middle Class School' and a 'Young Ladies Seminary'. For adult education there was the Mechanics Institute held in the Market House which had 134 members and 2000 books in its library.

The self-contained nature of the typical market town at this date is shown by the presence of fourteen shoemakers and thirty two people involved in making or selling clothes including the rather exotic Sarah Thomas who was a stay maker (i.e. corsets) and furrier in South Street. Other odd jobs listed include John Mills who produced ginger beer, soda and aerated water at his premises in Union Road. John Warwick described as 'book deliverer' and Frank Moore who was the town crier.

As befits a market town the agricultural sector was well represented with twenty eight farmers living within the town boundaries. Additionally there were ten dairies, wool, poultry, butter and seed dealers, sack and agricultural implement makers, malt-sters and even a 'cattle doctor'.

Last, and not least, were the publicans whose establishments ranged from the grand George Hotel to the humble beershop. If we include off-licences there were some thirty of these - approx-imately one per one hundred and thirty two inhabitants which suggests South Molton was a 'happy' place in 1879! *White's Directory* gives this information for every settlement in Devon which indicates how useful our own 'Yellow Pages' of today might be in a century's time. When the new ones come perhaps you should put the old one away in the loft as an heirloom for your descendants!

91. Ananias in Bideford

Education always seems to be in a state of flux. Today there are moves to grant ever greater freedom to head teachers to manage their own schools. When compulsory education was first intro-duced into Britain in the 1870s School Boards were set up to manage the newly created educational system. Members had to be elected on to these Boards and as always where there is democracy there were arguments - though few were as ran-corous as occurred at the Bideford School Board in August 1888.

Four members were present; R.Hookway, R.Dymond, H.L.Hutchings and H.Restarick, and the first item on the agen-da was the written resignation of the Reverend R.Granville. His letter was 'received without comment' and the chairman Mr.Hookway moved on to a motion put on the agenda by Mr.Hutchings.

Seen over the distance of more than a century the subject mat-ter appears a little esoteric but it had an explosive outcome. Hutchings was asking if the Attendance Officer (in charge of chasing up truants) Mr.Milsom actually examined the school registers himself? Before he got very far in introducing his motion Dymond declared that if the subject was to be discussed then it was only proper for the officer to explain in person how he did his job.

The chairman agreed and asked Milsom to answer the point. The officer said he did see the registers from which he drew up his 'lists of attendance' and teachers would usually highlight any 'particular bad case' they considered needed immediate action. This seemed to answer Hutchings' question but Dymond pointedly added that perhaps it would be better 'that the facts should be clearly ascertained' before any charges were made against an officer.

This seemed to be a red rag to a bull with Hutchings immediately losing his temper and exclaiming 'There's Ananias again. That man has told more lies since he entered the room, at this one meeting, than it was ever recorded Ananias and Saphira together ever told.' The two oddly named people were famous liars in the Bible and most people at this date would have probably been aware of the reference.

The chairman called Hutchings to order and as soon as he calmed down he proceeded to detail his evidence against Milsom. A boy named Hopgood had not attended school for two months he being 'unable to get his boots on' - yet Milsom had reported him present for most of this time.

Dymond, instead of looking at this case rose and demanded 'a total withdrawal of the unseemly expressions which had been made use of'. The chairman then reckoned that Hutchings 'would admit that he was altogether out of proper limits' and would withdraw 'the offensive expression'.

Hutchings, however, declined pointing out that a little time before Dymond had called him a 'murderer' and accused him of being on bad terms with every teacher in Bideford - yet Dymond had never withdrawn these comments. Hutchings then reverted to discussing Milsom but was again interrupted by Dymond demanding a retraction.

At this point the chairman said the meeting was becoming 'a beer garden' and called on Hutchings to apologise, which he again refused to do - a sequence repeated several times. In the words of the reporter 'the scene finally became of an exciting and painful character' with Hutchings 'excitedly declaring he never would withdraw his comments'. Poor Hookway clearly didn't know what to do next so he took the easiest way out and simply got up and left the meeting.

The next week's *Journal* carried a scathing anonymous letter which attacked the 'utter unfitness' of Hutchings to sit on the School Board and ended with the rousing call 'How long are the enlightened working men of Bideford going to tolerate Mr.Hutchings? It is hoped that the coming School Board election will emphatically answer this question in the right way, by send-ing Mr.Henry Lee Hutchings to 'Coventry'.' In fact he was returned - probably to the dismay of his fellow members if the foregoing is anything to go by! Colourful times for our ancestors yet one suspects the same sort of bickering still goes on at our own Parent-Teacher Associations and School Governors' meet-ings.

92. Road fever

In the nineteenth century no-one knew how diseases began. The scientific exploration of bacteria and viruses was yet to yield dis-coveries we take for granted today. The one thing our ancestors did know, however, was that diseases were infectious and suf-ferers had to be kept apart from the healthy if cross-infection was to be avoided.

Given this it is perhaps not that surprising to find a heading to a *Journal* article in 1894 that reads 'Removing a fever patient from Barnstaple to Torrington - Fined for exposing the patient.' The case behind this headline was heard at the Torrington Petty Sessions and concerned James Yeo a tailor of Barnstaple who had transported Frederick Thorne 'a person suffering from a dangerous infection' to the town. The prosecutor was George Doe the Torrington Town Clerk who was acting on information received from John Quick the 'Sanitary Inspector' employed by his council.

Yeo had previously lived in Torrington and Thorne had been his apprentice but on moving to Barnstaple the young lad had gone with his master. His parents had, however, made a 'special request' that 'if at any time he was taken ill he should remove him to his home at Torrington.'

The court heard how in December 1893 Thorne became ill but Yeo had put this down to his having eaten some unripe apples. After a spell in bed the boy got up, sat by the fire and Yeo and his wife gave him some brandy. Overnight, however, Thorne was sick - which his master didn't think surprising when he discovered the boy had filched and drunk a bottle of rhubarb wine! The boy remained ill yet twice refused to see a doctor.

Eventually Yeo put him on to his horse and trap and drove him back to his parents' house in Torrington not dreaming that he was seriously ill - indeed he thought he simply had a cold. His parents called in a Dr.Sutcliffe who immediately diagnosed that their son was 'suffering from scarlet fever in a severe form.' He reckoned that this should have been obvious to anyone and that by transporting him in an open cart the infection was liable to have been spread to others. In actual fact Thorne's brother had already caught it. John Thorne, the boy's father, was a local shepherd who deposed that his son didn't even recognise his mother when brought to her as he was so ill. John told Yeo that 'he ought to be ashamed of himself to remove the lad in that condition.'

The last witness called in the case was Frederick Stacey a Barnstaple cabinet maker who helped Yeo take the boy home. He didn't think there was anything seriously wrong with him and during the journey shared a bottle of brandy with him and lent him his coat - neither of which he would have done if he had thought him infected with any disease. He did have to admit that at one point the lad threw off his blanket apparently in a feverish state.

Faced with such evidence there could only be one decision. Yeo was clearly guilty but the magistrates believed he had only broken the law 'in ignorance' and so fined him the nominal sum of 1/- (5p). George Doe added the comment that it was a pity Barnstaple was not so careful as Torrington in dealing with such potentially serious cases of infection - a parting shot at another local authority in the days when local autonomy was jealously guarded.

North Devon Journal 7.10.1999

93. Rough times on Derby's Peace Day

In the book I co-authored *'Barnstaple's Vanished Lace Industry'* much space was taken up discussing the area in the town known as Derby. This was where most of the lacemakers lived and this industrial suburb was noted for its local customs and sense of community since its first development in the 1830s. The area was also, and not without reason, known as a fairly 'rough' area - as a story from 1919 shows.

On July 19 of that year Peace Day was celebrated throughout North Devon and that evening in Derby's Union Street Bessie Jones was standing on her doorstep awaiting the return of her husband and sons. Whilst she was there a young man called Bennett came along playing what was variously described as an accordion or melodeon. Behind him was a small group of his friends and acquaintances. Bessie asked him to stop 'for the sake of a poor old soul who was ill, and her sleeping baby.'

At this, two of the group, Florence Chapple and her father pushed their way into Bessie's house, knocked over a vase of flowers and 'smacked her in the face.' Hearing her mother's cries Bessie's daughter Gladys rushed downstairs and bundled the Chapples into the street. Here they began banging the door calling out 'most impudent names' and 'used most bad language' - not quite the behaviour one would have expected on Peace Day!

Bessie summonsed her attackers and in court Florence denied all the charges asking Bessie 'When did I touch you?' to which her victim replied, 'You were too drunk to remember' which seems to have made Florence lapse into silence. The musician Fred Bennett was then called and admitted that as he had come from Barnstaple town centre he had been 'keeping up a little jollification' As he approached the Jones' house Florence and her father began waltzing round to the 'swing of the music'. When Bessie Jones asked him to stop he immediately did so and went home - so not witnessing any assault.

The magistrates reached an immediate decision and fined Florence 10/- (50p) but she pleaded that 'as things were so dear she could not afford to pay for two months' - the magistrates, however, gave her two weeks to pay or else she would be gaoled.

Straight afterwards her parents James and Florence Chapple appeared to answer a charge of using 'bad language'. Bessie Jones once again gave her evidence but James leapt up to declare, 'It is a wonder that you do not drop dead in the box' adding 'You cannot get anything out of a liar.' Indeed he claimed that 'his missus went in and went to bed' without making any noise at all - to which Bessie retorted 'You had to pull her in though.'

Fred Bennett was again called but again claimed to have neither heard nor seen anything other than a 'jumble' of noise. Mrs Chapple ended the case by remarking that 'she could call neighbours to prove that I had no drink on Peace Day - and they were frightened.' This extremely ambiguous comment was greeted with roars of laughter in the court.

The magistrates were thus faced with conflicting evidence and so took the easy way out and dismissed the case - to the great relief of the Chapples. Colourful times in old Barnstaple which did nothing to dispel the reputation of Derby for neighbourly antagonism.

North Devon Journal 6.5.1999

94. Hartland's 'good old days'?

'Fifty years ago life in remote country districts was very different from what it is today.' So began a lecture delivered in 1922 by R.Pearse Chope, a noted antiquarian of Hartland, to the London Devonian Association.

Bearing in mind he was speaking of the 1870s it is perhaps surprising to read of Hartland that machinery was 'almost non-existent, wheeled vehicles had only recently come into use' whilst schools and postal deliveries were unknown. Each farm was virtually self-sufficient relying on the labour of the family and hired labourers.

These latter then earned 35p a week compared to the 35p a day they were earning in 1922 although they could buy cheap grain from their employer and were allowed 'a certain amount of manured potato ground' to cultivate for themselves. Only the head horseman and cowman got their cottage for free. Women were paid 4p a day for agricultural work although 'they only did such light work as hoeing, weeding, turning hay, and binding corn.' On these tiny incomes large families were brought up - the largest Chope remembered being a family of nineteen!

In times of unemployment life became very hard and Chope quotes from a petition of 1835 from the men of Hartland which described their low wages adding details such as 'many of us live from month to month without tasting any kind of meat or butter.' If ever they reared a pig it had to be sold to pay the rent on their cottages which was usually about £3 a year. They also complained about the system where the unemployed were 'sold' to local farmers for a fortnight at a time at a sort of public auction. If they refused to work they got no parish relief (dole) from the Overseer of the Poor who organised these auctions.

Chope moved on to describe the folk beliefs of his fellow parishioners. One Hartland girl reckoned that if, on Halloween, she stood in front of a mirror combing her hair and holding an apple the face of her future husband would appear over her shoulder - though presumably if no-one appeared she would assume that she was fated to remain a spinster?

Cider making began on All Saints Day and the best was considered to be the most acidic as this could 'cut the phlegm'. On Good Friday 'cock kibbiting' took place. A cock was placed under a clay milk pan and kibbits (or cudgels) were thrown at it until it broke. The first person to catch the cock then became its owner.

At Christmas kitchens were festooned with holly and laurel and a 'kissing bush' of furze studded with holly berries hung from the ceiling. A massive ash faggot bound with nine hazel 'bands' was then burnt in the hearth watched by the family along with their labourers. As each band burnt off the watchers would drink a quart of cider from small horn cups singing and telling jokes all the time - which sounds a custom worth bringing back.

One that definitely isn't was 'sparrow mumbling' where a boy had his hands tied behind him and the wing tip of a live sparrow put in his mouth. He then had to try and bite off the bird's head without it escaping - shades of Ozzy Osbourne!

Chope finished his talk with an account of local harvest customs which included 'making sweet hay'. Here a wisp of hay was twisted into a ring by a man and the prettiest girl in the harvest field kissed through it 'either with or without permission.' This was believed to make the hay crop 'sweet'. When getting corn in the whole of the parish worked from 'cocklight to dimmet' (dusk to dawn) to get the vital crop safely harvested. Five sustaining meals were taken during the day with all the workforce attending the huge harvest supper once the crop was gathered - which for many was the largest and richest meal they would have all year.

With mechanisation and compulsory education all of these old customs have gone - some we do not miss but others are perhaps worth reviving - and not just in Hartland.

North Devon Journal 22.7.1999

95. When the 'Black Shirts' came to North Devon

One of the more repellent episodes in the history of Britain this century was the rise of the fascist movement between the wars. Modelled on organisations started by Hitler and Mussolini the British Union of Fascists was founded in 1932 by Sir Oswald Mosley. Known, after their uniforms, as 'Blackshirts' they were largely an urban phenomenon but occasionally they were active in rural areas - as one such event from Buckland Brewer in 1933 demonstrates.

For many years farmers throughout the country had been grumbling about the system of tithes whereby they had to pay a sum of money to the Church Commissioners to support the parish clergy and church - whether they were members of the Church of England or not. In the 1930s their complaints came to a head and many refused to pay. The Church would then obtain a court order allowing bailiffs to enter the farms and seize goods to the value of the tithes owed.

Such heavy handed actions were, of course, extremely unpopular and the fascists saw them as a golden opportunity to win much needed support in country areas by sending their members to literally 'man the barricades' against the despised bailiffs.

In September 1933 an order was issued against L.W.Brown of Holwell Farm in Buckland Brewer for non-payment of tithes and advertisements were published saying that one rick of hay and two ricks of corn on the farm had been seized and were to be auctioned to pay off the debt. A court bailiff turned up to guard the ricks prior to their sale.

Only a week or so later the *Journal* reported that six young men turned up at the farm dressed in black shirts and flannel trousers. Along with them was R.A.Plathen the 'National Political Officer of the British Union of Fascists' who stated that their aim was to prevent the sale. He added that they were collecting signatures on a petition to the King in favour of altering the tithe system. The fascists had not been invited but the farmer didn't object to their help. The men began digging trenches across the approach road to the farm and 'had started barricading' whilst Plathen went off to address a 'Farmers' Meeting' at Shebbear on the iniquity of tithes.

Within days the two corn ricks 'mysteriously disappeared' along with part of the hay rick and the Court decided to send a second bailiff to defend what was left. It is said that 30 'Blackshirts' were involved in spiriting away the ricks. The first bailiff had been staying in the farmhouse but had to leave to direct the new man in. They arrived back to find the farm and outhouses padlocked up and the owner gone. Within minutes the new bailiff's case and parcel of provisions 'mysteriously disappeared' just like the ricks. Severe weather over the next few days meant the court officials had 'a trying ordeal' as 'they had no shelter from the wind and rain'.

The 'Blackshirts' in the meantime had partly cut through trees lining the road leading to the farm and these were 'roped ready to be dropped at a moment's notice as a further barricade' to any effort to enforce the auction notice.

Within a few days the Court admitted defeat and wrote to Farmer Brown saying they were stopping the action there being no point in carrying on. Only days after this fifty cases of non-payment of tithes were presented to the Court sitting at Torrington - but not one of the accused deigned to appear to answer the charges!

The 'Blackshirts' left for Plymouth after a few days on a lorry bearing two large signs. On the front was one reading 'Tithes - Bah' and on the back 'Victory from Buckland Brewer'. The publicity they obtained from this was excellent and was only spoilt by their later thuggery in the East End of London where their true Nazi sympathies were revealed.

Intriguingly a week after they left it was announced in the *Journal* that Mosley was considering purchasing Lundy as the Headquarters for his movement - a possibility he personally denied the following week. The whole episode was repeated a month later at Stoney Cross near Bideford when local farmer F.Chipman saw the 'Blackshirts' turn up to repel the bailiffs - as shown in the photograph.

North Devon Journal 20.4.2000

96. When *Woman's Hour* was broadcast from the New Inn at Bideford

Woman's Hour is a BBC staple listened to by millions. In its earlier years it often did outside broadcasts from various locations in Britain and in February 1958 Bideford was chosen. A script was prepared and very luckily one has survived which recently came into my possession. This shows that a temporary studio was set up at the New Inn in the town - from where nine people were interviewed.

First up was Alfred Blackwell, the librarian of the North Devon Athenaeum in Barnstaple, who spoke on 'What Instow means to me' he having written a small booklet on the village. Blackwell began by recounting how he had come to Instow 21 years before and how much he enjoyed the 'trim villas and green shutters on cream-coloured facades' of the village. He went on to recount the history of the Torridge estuary including the rebuilding of the schooner *Rylands* as the *Hispaniola* galleon at Appledore prior to its starring part in the film *Treasure Island*. After filming the ship apparently left the estuary flying the Jolly Roger flag.

The next speaker was Katherine Tottenham who also lived in Instow and was the local RSPCA officer. She discussed the problem of seabirds getting covered in oil - even 40+ years ago this was a local problem though she did not make it clear how widespread the problem was.

She was followed by Miss Abbott, the 80-year old redoubtable ex-headmistress of West Bank School in Bideford (which later became Grenville College and is now part of Kingsley College). She discussed her childhood in Frithelstock, where her family had farmed for some 400 years. This included a description of a claustrophobic sounding horse-drawn cart used by the unmarried women in her family where the only ventilation was through a small aperture in the front - 'only opened when one of my Aunties wanted to speak to the driver'.

Then came Robert Harper, who had been selling books in Bideford for 50 years and had amassed a stock of some 50,000 titles. He told of the difficulties of running a bookshop in a small town where sometimes customers 'commanded' him to stop selling books they didn't like including the *Intelligent Woman's Guide to Socialism* by George Bernard Shaw and various titles by D.H.Lawrence!

Next up was Miss Eardley-Wilmot, who was the daughter of an ex-Indian Army Colonel who had retired to Westward Ho! just after it was established. She recalled the resort being full of Generals and Admirals - a whole military society in miniature.

After a short interlude with a Miss Darnley-Naylor of Northam, who translated Italian short stories, the programme came up to date with interviews with P.Fletcher and W.Whiteland who discussed the 'Two New Bideford Industries' they were involved with. The former was manufacturing newly introduced plastic baby pants and, when asked about available colours, he replied rather oddly 'For British babies, lavender, pink, blue and sometimes lemon. But for export babies, lavender, turquoise and nil as well.' The latter gentleman produced tooling equipment and explained how many of his workers had come to North Devon 'as a result of Government dispersal schemes during the war.'

The last speaker was Percy Harris of Appledore Shipbuilders who told the story of how, when his father P.K.Harris, was asked 'Where do you go for your holidays?' would simply look across the Torridge and reply, 'Look, what do I want to go away for?

I've been all over the world, is there a lovelier sight than that?'
On that very positive note the broadcast drew to a close. I do not
know whether a recording of the event still remains in the BBC
archives but it would be exciting to know it does.
North Devon Journal 5.4.2001

97. The Exmoor Beast

No other story, perhaps in recent years has so caught the public's
attention as that of the Exmoor Beast. From the first notice in the
Journal-Herald on April 21 1983 it has been a source of unending
argument and speculation. The main points of the story are that
in Spring 1982 rumours started that a large black animal was
responsible for the death of 10 lambs at Drewston Farm, near
South Molton. The killer apparently returned the next spring
when 30 lambs were lost, some disappearing without trace and
others being found 'stripped almost clean of flesh.'

The *Journal-Herald* front-page story covering this second batch
of deaths was copied by many other papers and alerted local
people to be on the lookout for unusual animals. From this date
the reports began to flood in. The animal was seen by a 16 year
old girl, a school bus driver, an ambulance driver, farmers and
even one of the Marine snipers brought in to try and track down
the Beast. This rash of sightings was followed by the offer of a
£1000 reward by a national newspaper for an authentic photograph of 'whatever it was', an offer that has never been taken up.

The sightings and killings continued being reported from over
the border into Somerset and down near the Cornish border as
well. After the final sightings in Spring of this year, the Beast
appears to have gone leaving us none the wiser as to what it was
or wasn't, and we have been left with two questions; why did it
suddenly appear - and what could it have been?

Reports of strange black creatures variously likened to large
black dogs or cats have been noted for hundreds of years in
North Devon. Perhaps the most famous is the Black Dog of
Frithelstock or Torrington, an animal generally dismissed as part
of the area's folklore, but one which bears an uncanny resem-
blance to our Beast. The last sighting of this animal was in 1982

when a past Mayor of Bideford, Fred Bailey, claimed he saw a strange dog-like thing as he was returning home late at night near Bideford.

At the start of the Beast story in 1983, two building workers said they had seen 'a large black cat-like animal' near Drewston Farm in previous years. Other big cats have been seen around South Devon in the late 1970's and early 1980's and I was recently given a record of a sighting from 40 years ago. This occurred at Horns Cross around 1943/44 when Bill and May Thornton, then doing wartime agricultural work, saw what they described as a strange black creature. The record of their sighting reads as follows:

> 'Early one Sunday morning my wife went to the window and drew back the curtains to look out at the weather. She called me very excitedly that there was a very strange animal coming up across the land opposite. It was at our estimate about 3 feet in height and possibly 4 feet in length, with thick heavy legs and appeared to be smooth coated and square headed. My wife who had first sighting, said it was a black animal. I can only say it was a very dark animal, because as it was moving up to the main road the red rising sun shone on it and made alterations to the depth of colour.'

His description tallies in most ways with recent sightings. At the time he actually told the farmer whom he was working for - who, 'expressed no great excitement and said he had at times seen it and his father before him' remarking that they knew it as the 'black dog' Apparently, 'The farmer was a fine steady type and certainly not superstitious, and that made the situation more real to us.'

What is intriguing, of course, is that sightings such as this one extend the life of the Beast at least 40 or more years, far too long for one Beast which suggests that there must be enough of them to constitute a breeding population. Whatever the truth of matter, we do seem to have found the answer to one of our questions; the Beast did not suddenly appear but it, or they, have been in the area for many years.

As to the second question - what is it? - we are on shakier ground. Lots of possibilities have been put forward; rogue dog, Tasmanian tiger, panther, African badger, wolf, lion, lynx and even a phantom! Only the capture of a Beast will settle the question once and for all, though the possibility of catching one seems remote. On the present evidence we can, however, make one or two suggestions.

With regard to a rogue dog it seems unlikely, given the unusual method of killing adopted by the beast which apparently is alien to dogs though not to cats. A member of the cat family would appear to be a better candidate. A large cat, such as a puma or lion, would surely be very obvious and if there is a breeding population would certainly have been noted before now. Having said this, it should be recalled that large cats have turned up in North Devon. Who remembers the two dead lions that were found at Fremington abattoir and were never claimed several years ago?

Another large cat is recorded in the *North Devon Journal* for 1868 where a report was printed about the escape of a 'Tasmanian devil' at Bideford which was on the loose for some days before being recaptured. Other escapes from similar travelling zoos might not have been caught or, indeed, this one may have bred in its few days of freedom. Its techniques of killing by directly chopping into the skull of its victims with its powerful jaws was seen several times in the killings put down to the Beast. Di Francis in her recent book *'Cat Country'* put forward an intriguing claim that Britain harbours an as yet undescribed type of large cat and supports her case with photographs and personal sightings. She now produces a magazine listing such cat sightings in Britain.

One other type of cat is a possibility for the Beast - the British wild cat. The last written record of wild cats in North Devon comes from Exmoor in 1283 but there has been a strong oral tradition up until the early twentieth century that the wild cat bred on a particular hill on the moor. Indeed, Fred Milton, past president of the Exmoor Pony Society claims to have see one and his record appears in Hope Bourne's *'Living on Exmoor'*. He describes it as 'about the size of a dog fox. In colour it was grey or tawny grey, marked all over with dark stripes. Its head was huge in comparison with that of an ordinary cat, and its teeth protruded below the lip like fangs. Its tail was thick and blunt and hung in a distinctive curve behind it. The creature seemed tall in the leg, especially in the hind quarters, and it moved with a sort of slouching gait.'

Anthony Dent in his *'Lost Beasts of Britain'* suggests that the wild cat could still survive on Exmoor and, for what it is worth, I would nominate a type of British wild cat as the Exmoor Beast, a great rarity that should be conserved rather than shot or captured - except on film.

[A version of this first appeared in the *North Devon Journal-Herald* 4.10.1984]

98. The early history of the *Bideford Gazette*

The very first issue of the *Gazette* appeared in Bideford on the 1st of January 1856 under the imposing title *The Devon and East Cornwall Gazette and Commercial Advertiser*. It was one of a whole number of provincial papers that began around this time following the removal of a tax on newspapers which had kept their price artificially high. In addition new mechanical paper making techniques had made supplies of newsprint far cheaper.

The *Gazette*'s first publisher/printer/editor was Thomas Honey a 26 year old bookseller who had decided to broaden his business interests by starting a local paper. He was based in Grenville Street (then known as Market Hill) in Bideford and had only been working on his own behalf for some 3 years having purchased his bookselling business in November 1853 from Messrs.Johnson and Cole who themselves had taken it on from John Hayman in January 1852. Intriguingly Hayman had only sold it when he moved to Barnstaple to take over the *North Devon Journal*. Possibly it was this movement into newspaper publishing that inspired Honey to give it a try. However he got into the business he was very proud of his new newspaper.

In the first issue he wrote 'On making our first appearance before the public, in this form, and on the very day when we pass from the old year to the new, we cannot but feel the responsibility that must attach itself to us; and in the arduous time that lies before us, we shall endeavour honestly to discharge our duties.' Striking a business note he added 'To Correspondents - The Editor is not responsible for the Contents of Correspondent's letters' and 'We cannot undertake to return rejected communications'.

Thomas, however, knew where his economic interests lay for he also wrote 'Advertisers are respectfully reminded of the advantages of this Paper as an advertising medium. It is circulated widely in North Devon and East Cornwall. The terms for advertising are very low, and will receive prompt and careful attention on being sent to T.Honey, Printer &c, Bideford.' Thomas published a list of those who were selling his new venture with agents as far apart as Stratton, Holsworthy and Chulmleigh. Interestingly these people included an ironmonger, schoolmaster and a butcher - clearly Victorians turned their hands to many things.

The first number of the *Gazette* actually only carried 10 advertisements but business soon picked up and a few even boasted an engraving to attract the eye. Thus Pridham & Lake, coach proprietors, headed their advertisements with a stirring picture of a coach and four galloping horses. The Bideford-Exeter railway service used a charming if slightly odd looking drawing of a very early train with a freight truck piled high with boxes and bags whilst a fairly nondescript ship headed the advertisement for an emigrants' ship to America. The most unusual of these early advertisements is headed 'A Photographic Portrait For One Shilling' which was being offered by two London based photographers. One wonders how many of these very early photographs have survived?

These first *Gazettes* consisted of a large double sheet folded in two to make 4 pages. Three of these were printed elsewhere (probably in Exeter) with only the front page carrying local news and adverts. Thomas does not appear to have had any reporters but relied on friends sending him information. By June 1856 the name of the paper had been changed to *The Bideford Weekly Gazette and Devon and Cornwall Advertiser* - its full title until 1909.

The new business flourished and we can imagine how proud Thomas and his wife Eliza must have been to insert the birth notice of their daughter Mary in the issue of 19th June. Sadly, however, at some time in 1856 Thomas fell ill and in issue No.48 of 25th November appeared the following death notice, '21st inst, at Market Hill, Bideford, after a long and painful illness which he bore with Christian resignation, Mr Thomas Honey, printer, and publisher of this *Gazette*, aged 27.' He was buried in the Bideford Old Town Cemetery and a small inscribed stone marks his last resting place.

Poor Eliza was aged just 25 and had a 5 month old baby, and doubtless most people thought the *Gazette* would either have to close or be sold. Eliza, however, was made of stern stuff and amazingly decided to carry on the young publication - a decision she announced in the edition that appeared on 16th December. A week later the *Gazette* carried a small advertisement, 'Wanted, a respectable FEMALE SERVANT, one who can undertake the charge of a Baby - Apply at the Office of this Paper. A Wesleyan preferred.' Clearly Eliza was a Methodist who had decided that her late husband's newspaper should come before her child. Knowing how fiercely patriarchal Victorian society was we can only marvel at Eliza's courage at becoming the only female newspaper editor in nineteenth-century England of whom I am aware.

In fact the *Gazette* went from strength to strength and Eliza found time to carry on the bookselling side of the business as well as handling a variety of one-off printing jobs. Thus in 1857 she was advertising for a book binder to work for her whilst in 1858 she printed a book of poems by a local Wesleyan minister. In the same year she let it be known that she could take on an apprentice to learn the trade - a post that was re-advertised in 1862 and 1863. The advertisement reproduced between pages 96-97 gives some idea of the books she was selling at this time - solid literature and religious works though notice the reference to her being the local agent for the Crown Life Insurance Co. In fact Eliza also sold patent medicines and umbrellas along with various stationery goods - a not unusual grouping of goods at this date.

Over the first decade of the *Gazette*'s existence Eliza advertised fairly regularly on her own behalf. In 1857, for example, she was offering musical instruments for sale, in 1862 she was selling 'shop soiled books', Valentines were sold in January for many years whilst in 1863 she was selling the *Daily Telegraph* cheap - on the day after its publication!

In 1862 she tried to sell her building in Grenville Street. Possibly it was too big for her or she wanted to move to a more central location? Whatever the reason the advert reproduced here shows the premises to have been a very substantial property - whilst the claim that it had been a printing/bookshop for 50 years is intriguing.

In the same year she was advertising for a 'Strong active man' to work for her for 2-3 hours a week in the newspaper office which, taken in conjunction with her attempted property sale, suggests Eliza might have been finding the strain of producing a weekly newspaper becoming too much. She seems to have carried on, however, though a court case from May 1867 shows her in a less than sympathetic light. Her apprentice Abraham Kingdon took her to court alleging 'he had not been taught the arts of printing and bookbinding according to the terms of his indenture.' A legal wrangle saw the case being adjourned for 2 weeks but it never came to be heard - probably Eliza settled with her aggrieved employee out of court.

We get a glimpse of Eliza through the eyes of one of her apprentices Harry Sanguin who wrote his memoirs in 1926. He had been born in Bideford and was apprenticed to Eliza in 1870. At this time 'the office was a small but fairly efficient place and the paper was a four-page sheet two of which (containing national news) were printed in London. The remaining two pages were printed in the office.' Harry's job was to help produce these 2 pages on a hand press which Harry reckoned (in something of an understatement) to be 'quite a laborious job.'

In September 1875 after 19 years Eliza retired and handed over the business to her relative William Honey who was then 39. William ran the paper with just 3 'boys' (one of them his son) to help. He clearly did not have the staying power or business acumen of Eliza as in June 1879 the *North Devon Journal* carried a small paragraph under its 'Bideford' news that read, 'A petition in Bankruptcy has been filed in the Barnstaple County Court by Mr. W.J. Honey, of this town, printer, newspaper proprietor and publisher, stationer etc. The debts are said to be about £1300. The first meeting is fixed for the 30th inst.'

At this meeting further details came out concerning Honey's failure. He had started in the business 'with little or no capital' and had, indeed, to mortgage his house and business to a John Fry for £850 - at 7% interest. Within 6 months he defaulted on his repayments claiming that 'trade had been very depressed at Bideford'. The breakdown of his debts showed he owed £437 to various creditors as well as £921 to Fry. In terms of assets his house was valued at £600 - whilst stock-in-trade was valued at £100, book debts £160, a bank balance of £3.5.0, furniture £25, printing press and type £200 and cash in hand £19. Clearly he couldn't pay his creditors so he offered them 5/- in the £ payable in three instalments. After some wrangling the creditors agreed to this which allowed Honey to continue the paper to try and drum up a more regular income.

Obviously this situation couldn't go on and in June 1882 Honey was asking his subscribers to support the new owner of the *Gazette* W.Crosbie Coles. The new owner lost no time in appointing new staff as in 1882 he took on John Redcliffe, the son of James, a Bideford potter, as an apprentice. Mr.Coles clearly wanted value for money as John's wages were to be 3/- (15p) per week in his first year rising, after 4 years, to the dizzying height of 7/- (35p) per week - the working week 'not to exceed sixty hours'! Within a short time Coles went into partnership with a Mr.Lee, an arrangement that lasted for many years even following Coles' retirement to Kent in 1894.

The *Gazette* office continued to print for others. In 1883 for example it printed the 'History of Bideford' by the Rev.Roger Granville, 1894 saw a guidebook 'Kingsley's Country' issued and in 1925 the 'Story of the Long Bridge of Bideford' by Clive Holland was printed. As the new century dawned James Owen was the editor of the paper and the *Gazette* embarked on various local takeovers. In 1901 it bought the *Western Times* and in 1911 the *Western Express and Torrington Chronicle* and thus solidified its position with local newspaper buyers. This then was the first 50 years of the *Gazette*'s life in which its owners overcame large obstacles to become a fixed part of the North Devon landscape.

References

1. *Calendar of Close Rolls* published by PRO
2. *Transactions of the Devonshire Association* Vol 45 1913 pp.455-478
3. North Devon Journal (NDJ) 19.11.1846 2d, 26.11.1846 3f, 18.2.1847 2g, 25.3.1847 2f-g
4. NDJ 18.4.1850 8e
5. NDJ 12.7.1855 8a, 2.8.1855 8d
6. *Report of the Commissioners to inquire into the existence of corrupt practices in the Borough of Barnstaple.* HMSO 1853
7. NDJ 5.5.1870 7b
8. NDJ 4.8.1870 4e-f + 5a-f
9. NDJ 7.3.1912 3c
10. Bideford Gazette (BG) 16.4.1901 5c
11. NDJ 17.3.1910 8b-c
12. NDJ 25.8.1910 7c, 4.8.1910 3d
13. NDJ 11.9.1924 8b
14. NDJ 18.8.1938 4d-e
15. North Devon Record Office (NDRO) - BBT/B6/1
16. NDRO - B/1 3996
17. NDRO - BBT/A2/1-3
18. NDJ 8.11.1855 5b-d
19. NDJ 17.7.1856 3b-c
20. NDJ 20.8.1857 8d-e
21. NDJ 5.4.1894 8b-c
22. NDJ 27.6.1861, 4.7.1861
23. NDJ 12.3.1903 5c-d
24. NDJ 26.1.1865 7b-c
25. NDJ 18.11.1905
26. NDJ 20.1.1870 6e-f
27. *Return of Owners of land in England and Wales* 1872-3. HMSO Parliamentary Paper 1874
28. In my personal possession
29. NDJ 22.7.1886 2c-d
30. NDJ 16.2.1899 2a-b
31. NDJ 8.2.1906 8a-d
32. NDJ 18.7.1907 6b-d
33. NDJ 13.10.1910 7a-c

34. In my personal possession
35. NDJ 26.4.1934 5d-e
36. NDJ 8.12.1836 4d-e, 15.12.1836 1e
37. NDJ 3.3.1859 5e
38. NDJ 9.5.1867 5e-f
39. NDRO 1843A/PX23
40. NDJ 25.6.1885 8a-b
41. NDJ 13.4.1899 6c-d
42. NDJ 30.3.1905 8b-c
43. *Devon Muster Roll of 1569* by A.J.Howard & T.L.Stoate 1977
44. NDRO R2379/Z38
45. NDJ 12.6.1856 8a-b
46. NDJ 16.5.1907 2d
47. NDJ 21.6.1860 5e-f
48. NDJ 27.6.1861 5e-f
49. NDRO R2379A/Z32
50. *Of Chirche-Reves, and of Testamentes. The Church, Sex and Slander in Elizabethan North Devon* P.Christie, Devon Family History Society 1994
51. NDRO 3253 A-1
52. NDJ 20.10.1856 5a
53. NDJ 21.2.1867 6c, 28.2.1867 5f, 7.3.1867 8e
54. NDJ 16.12.1875 5f
55. NDJ 7.3.1878 8c, 21.3.1878 8b, 4.4.1878 8e, 23.5.1878 3a
56. NDJ 25.9.1879 8c-d, 2.10.1879 8b, 9.10.1879 8c, 16.10.1879 8a-b, 23.10.1879 8b, 6.11.1879 8b, 20.11.1879 8d, 27.11.1879 8a-e, 11.12.1879 8c
57. NDJ 4.9.1884 8c
58. NDJ 31.5.1906 3a-c
59. NDJ 1.5.1851 4c-d
60. NDJ 21.7.1853 5b-c, 28.7.1853 5a
61. NDJ 24.8.1854 5c, 21.9.1854 6d
62. NDJ 6.12.1855 5c, 13.12.1855 p.2, p.3,5d
63. NDJ 25.9.1856 2a-c
64. NDJ 5.11.1857 5e-f
65. NDJ 26.10.1865 5d-e
66. NDJ 11.3.1869 6a-b
67. NDJ 9.6.1892 5f, 16.6.1892 2e-f
68. NDJ 16.11.1933 p.2
69. NDJ 22.6.1899 6e
70. NDJ8.2.1912 2a-d
71. NDRO 1892 A add 2/ PO 556-607

72. NDRO 3253 add A/ PV1, PO5
73. NDRO 2939/A/PO12-15
74. NDRO 1794A/PW
75. NDRO 2044A/PO3
76. *Devon Extracts From The London Gazette* (2 vols: 1665-1765, 1665-1850), Marjorie Snetzler (transcr.), Devon Family History Society 1987
77. Copies are housed in the North Devon Athenaeum
78. Various NDJ
79. NDJ 11.7.1912 3d
80. NDJ 4.1.1844 2f + 3d
81. NDJ 25.5.1850 4b
82. NDJ 7.11.1850 4d-e
83. NDJ 30.4.1857 8a
84. NDJ 16.4.1857 5d-e
85. NDJ 5.3.1868 8a + 8d, 12.3.1868 8a
86. NDJ 11.5.1871 5d-f
87. NDJ 2.10.1873 8e, 27.11.1873 5f, 4.12.1873 5e-f, 11.12.1873 2b-c, 19.3.1874 6e
88. NDJ 10.6.1873 5b
89. NDJ 9.4.1874 2a
90. *White's Directory of Devon* 1879
91. NDJ 6.9.1888 6c-d
92. NDJ 1.2.1894 5d
93. NDJ 7.8.1919 7b
94. BG 7.3.1922 7d-e
95. NDJ 5.10.1933 5g, 12.10.1933 7d-e, 26.10.1933 2f, 2.11.1933 3g
96. In my personal possession
97. NDJ various + in my personal possession
98. NDJ + BG various

INDEX

Cadd, Richard 36
Caddy, Edmund 85
Caldey Island 68
Canderton, Alexander 8
Cann, Abraham 150
Cann, John 51
Cann, Mary 143
Cann, Thomas 138
Carder, Miss 165
Carders, William 36
Carnegie, Andrew 62
Carnegie, C.S. 63
Casinelli, Sarah 132
Cawsey, Ellen 157
Cawsey, Henry 111
Cawsey, John 39
Cawsey, P.c. 92
Challacombe 28,153
Challacombe, Hannah 139
Challacombe, William 151
Chanter, C.E. 26
Chanter, J.R. 148
Chanter, Major 85
Chanter, P.c. 116
Chanter, T 21
Chapple, Florence 176
Chapple, James 176
Charles 103
Chicheley, William 7
Chichester, Sir Francis 74
Chichestre, Richard 7
Chile 75
Chipman, F 181
Chittlehampton 20,147
Chope, R.P. 177
Chulmleigh 138,151,187
Clark, John 100
Clarke, Captain Gould 135
Clarke, Thomas 126
Cleveland, J 147
Cleverdon, Henry 137
Clinton, Lord 63
Clogg, Edward 138,140
Clouteman, John 32
Clovelly 9,12,81,82,85
Cock, J.W. 24
Cock, Roger 142
Cockram, Abraham 147
Cole, James 154
Cole 186
Coles, W.Crosbie 190
Colking 151
Collacott, Elizabeth 141
Colley, Thomas 85
Combe Martin 49,118,121

Cook, Captain 29
Cook, Dr. 169
Cooke, Dr. 158
Cooke, Michael 116
Cork 81
Cotton, G.K. 102
Couch, John 80
Countisbury 101,152
Courtney 139
Crang, Michael 85
Cream, Dr.Thomas 129
Crawshaw 59
Creek, William 122
Crimea 38,86
Cross, Sam 100
Cross, William 140
Croyde 168
Cudmore, Patrick 97
Cummins, Mr. 169
Cutcliffe, John 154
Dadds 49
Dark, Captain 57,80
Darnell, Mr. 13
Darnley-Naylor, Miss 182
Davis, Frederick 80
Davis, Geoffrey 99
Davis, Joseph 82
Davy, John 14
Day, Captain Thomas 71
Dendle, Ann 122
Denmark 46
Dennis, George 32
Dennis, Philip 119
Dennis, Robert 33
Dent, Anthony 186
Devonport 92
Doe, George 174
Dornat 112
Dowell, Admiral 76
Down, George 33
Downe, Edward 98
Downe, Elizabeth 98
Dowsett, J.H. 162
Dublin 73
Dummett, Robert 74
Dunford, James 99
Dunkirk 93
Dunn, A 62
Dyer, Ernest 135
Dyer, George 99
Dyer, Mary 99
Dyer, Philip 116
Dymond, R 172
Eardley-Wilmot, Miss 182
Eastdown 124

Heaven, Miss 58
Hedden, John 85
Henckley, Mr. 27
Henry VI 8
Herapath, William 122
Herley, Elizabeth 154
Hewitt, William 23
Hill, Thomas 52
Hill, William 91
Hitler 179
Hodsoll, Ann 117
Hogg, Captain 126
Hole, John 146
Hole, Robert 121
Holland 8
Holland, Clive 190
Holmes, Edwin 20
Holsworthy 41,85,128,187
Honey, Eliza 186
Honey, Mary 186
Honey, Thomas 186
Honey, William 186
Hookway, R 172
Hooper 86
Hooper, David 71
Hooper, S 87
Hooper, W 152
Hopgood 173
Hopkins, William 99
Horns Cross 184
Horwood 160
Hoyle, Thomas 126
Hughs, William 100
Hutchings, H.L. 172
Huxtable, George 164
Huxtable, Joseph 125
Huxtable, William 104

Ilfracombe
11,23,48,55,57,63,73,80,97,128,133,138,150,151
Inder, Mabel 68
India 88
Instow 57,71,76,78,80,160,181
Ireland, Mr. 164
Italy 30

Jackson, L 94
Jackson, Dr.Mark 59
Jamaica 31,92
Jeffery, P.Sergt 134
Jenkin, Edward 32
Jenner, Edward 139
Jewell 151
Jewell, James 121
Jewell, Margaretta 154

Jewell, Robert 154
Johnson 186
Joliffe, John 137
Jones, Bessie 176
Jones, Captain 81
Jones, Eliza 116
Jones, P.c.George 92
Jones, Gladys 176
Jones, John 65
Jones. Lt. 74
Jones, Lucy 109

Keene, H 89
Kellaway, Lemon 166
Kentisbury 150
Kingdon, Abraham 189
Kingdom, Sergt.T 89
Kingdon, Rev.Roger 42
Kingsley, Charles 48,61
Kingsnympton 147
Knowstone 147

Lake 139,187
Lake, John 107
Lamprey, John 165
Lamprey, Mrs. 165
Landcross 81,84
Landkey 69
Lapford 147
Lawrence, D.H. 182
Lawrence, Richard 99
Lee, Agnes 143
Lee, Christian 137
Lee, Mr. 190
Lee, Robert 143
Leitheby, Charity 143
Lethaby, Mrs. 113
Leverton, Frances 145
Leverton, Mr. 164
Lewis, Ann 140
Lewis, William 145
Liteljohn, John 96
Liverpool 14
London 12,19,29,36,74,107,129,153,181,189
Longman, Mary 144
Loosemore, James 143
Lundy 26,57,64,80,181
Luxmoore, Rev.Henry 38,102
Lynmouth 24
Lynton 40,49,150,152

Madge, George 145
Madge, Mary 145
Major, William 36
Manning 124

197